Come Together

The Architecture of
Multigenerational Living

gestalten

Table of Contents

TOGETHER

Around the world, multiple generations are finding new ways to live together.

UNDER

ONE

ROOF

Left
Flexible, inclusive design has been encouraging a new wave of multigenerational living, from Australia to Amsterdam.

Just over a century ago, a family spanning multiple generations living under one roof was nothing worth writing a book about. A house shared by grandparents, parents, and grandchildren, and sometimes aunts and uncles too, was the norm, a way of life. With the rise of the nuclear family following World War II came a growing desire for independence—and with it the rise of the suburbs and the single family home as the abode of choice in many areas of the western world.

But, more than fifty years on, there is change afoot. Rising real estate prices outpacing the average income in many cities have made it near impossible for young families to buy homes. It's one of the leading causes that young people stay with their parents, or return after university or even later in life. It's not just affecting the younger generation, but their grandparents, too. According to the UN, by 2050, one in six people in the world will be over 65, but we're already seeing today how the growing aging population lacks affordable and quality care. Together, it's a perfect storm that has led multiple generations from Europe to Asia and Australia to reconsider the shared home as a viable solution to some of today's most pressing problems.

It's important to note upfront that multigenerational housing is a choice for some, but for many more it's a decision made out of economic necessity. Some families are forced into it down the line, while for others it has always been the only affordable option. To ignore this fact would be naive. In the same vein, it's also important to acknowledge that many of the houses featured in this book are high-end, architect-designed homes that are likely out of reach for many. But that shouldn't undermine them: they serve as sources of inspiration of what's possible under one roof. For those who are choosing to live together, and have the privilege to commission custom-designed dwellings, multigenerational living is embraced for its benefits, including shared costs, shared care, and the opportunity to build bonds.

"It's definitely brought us together," says Anne Heinl, who shares a home with her husband, son and daughter-in-law, and their two children in Victoria, British Columbia. Adapting multigenerational living to the twenty-first century, architects are delivering designs that don't only balance interdependence and independence—they're also especially easy on the eyes. "With just a few strategic, carefully conceived moves you can actually have this great connection but also separation when you need it. That's the trick," says architect Andrew Maynard, founding principal of Austin Maynard Architects, which has built a number of multigen homes in Australia, where multigenerational living is particularly on the rise.

The shared home has moved leaps and bounds from the ubiquitous granny flat, a self-contained unit that previously was most commonly associated with multigenerational living. Changing household make-up and their collective concerns have fueled a need for a new type of housing to accommodate them, and architects around the world →

are stepping up to the task to design living arrangements that suit a fluid generational mix.

Near the sea in Vaux-sur-Mer, France, TICA architectes et urbanistes' 2 en 1 House merges two homes into one single dwelling. Here, two sides, one slightly larger, flow in one long line with a central common space creating a connection point between the two and distinguishing them on the north-facing side. In Melbourne, Austin Maynard's Charles House exemplifies multigenerational homes with an integrated granny flat. Weaved into a ground floor section of the sprawling slate and timber clad home, the space that can easily adapt from a communal living space to a self-contained apartment, allowing the grandparents to be part of the household while remaining independent. Another example, Leckie Studio's Full House in Vancouver, is a five-bedroom home in its default mode, but can easily change configurations to accommodate the family.

Different as their approaches may be, multigenerational houses must all juggle private and common space, accessible and inclusive design for different abilities and ages, and the flexibility to accommodate the comings and goings of all residents. Rooms that are currently occupied by young children are designed to easily expand into studio-like spaces if they return home as young adults. Sliding doors or doors that can seamlessly blend into existing walls can transform a single family home into a duplex, or a triplex, to accommodate grandparents and other family members through the various stages of their lives. When not in use, different parts of the home can be sectioned off into rentable living and office spaces, generating income for the residents. Regardless of their unique design details, material palettes, and connection to their particular surroundings, these homes are designed to evolve with the generations and even beyond them. These core ingredients—flexibility, inclusivity, and separation between common and private spaces—are the factors that make these homes a success.

Architects and homeowners alike often look to Asia as a source of inspiration and a historical reference point, where the engrained tradition of multigenerational living goes back centuries. Rooted in long-standing →

Right
Shotgun Chameleon, designed by ZDES architects in Houston, Texas, is part of a growing international movement towards multigenerational living.

"With just a few strategic, carefully conceived moves you can actually have this great connection but also separation when you need it. That's the trick."

Top left
A new vision of multigenerational living in Asia features modernist and practical designs, such as Wall House by CTA Creative Architects in Vietnam.

Bottom left
House of Generations in Aarhus brings together seniors, families, people with disabilities, and the younger generations.

Confucian principles of filial piety—the expectation that the young will take care of their elders—the tradition has carried on in some countries and changed form in others. Beyond East Asia and Southeast Asia, multigenerational living has also been part of the norm in places like India and Iran, and the Middle East. This is also the case in parts of Europe, including Italy where children tend to live with their parents longer. As a result of growing immigration, the tradition has also traveled beyond borders to countries like Australia, America, and Canada.

Although the terms multigenerational and intergenerational are often used interchangeably, in this book we use the latter to distinguish multifamily homes, compared to single family homes shared by the same family. Beyond multigenerational living shared by families, intergenerational community living is also making a comeback. Some of the most notable projects are coming out of Denmark; including the House of Generations in Aarhus, where seniors, young families, students, and people with disabilities are mixed together in what architect Claus Jensen of Copenhagen-based RUM architects calls "a melting pot." It's no wonder, as one version of modern coliving is accepted to have originated in Denmark in the 1970s. Called *bofællesskab*, these living communities began with Sættedammen, a housing community of 27 units and shared common space, established by 35 families in 1972.

Of course, multigenerational living in all its forms dates back much further. "For most of history, the dominant form of living was communal, cooperative, and multigenerational," states the introduction to a timeline of collective architecture in *Together! The New Architecture of the Collective*, a catalog accompanying the eponymous exhibition held at the Vitra Museum of Design in 2017. "Prehistoric cavemen lived not as nuclear families, but rather as 'hordes' of extended family members; countless traditional housing typologies from the Hakka Tulou to the Roman domus, were meant for multiple families to live together in communion." It wasn't until the industrial age that many families moved away from multigenerational living. Previously dependent on an agrarian economy that allowed family members to live together throughout their lifecycles to care for the land and one another, the nineteenth century saw extended family units break up into smaller groupings and the young leaving their homesteads and multigenerational village communities for new opportunities in the city.

Embraced as a new model for living, today's multigenerational lifestyle offers dignified living for all generations. The young can learn from the old, the old can be energized by the young, and working parents can have a break. "It's a long time coming to start to have these conversations," says architect Betsy Williamson, principal of Toronto-based Williamson Williamson. What the homes featured in this book show is that through carefully considered design, it's possible to live your own life and share it with others all under one roof. •

Living Independently Together

Project
Copper Lane

Designer
Henley Halebrown

Location
London, U.K.

A former kindergarten block has been radically transformed into the city's first cohousing project: Copper Lane provides an affordable model for communal living, while supporting an intentional community of families. The six groups, who previously did not all know each other, pooled money together to buy the land and build six individual houses with communal spaces to share. The cluster of homes is arranged around a central courtyard positioned on the aboveground floor, with a continuous perimeter of communal gardens that wraps around the property. This gives each home the opportunity to have balconies and windows that face into the courtyard, while other areas face toward the gardens, allowing privacy. Compared to typical London terraced houses where the public eye cannot see beyond the front door, the boundaries between public and private at Copper Lane go further than the norm, while still providing balance and seclusion. "It shows how architecture can respond to a new social need that has arisen through changes in both lifestyles and economics," the firm explains.

→

Communal Space

The aim of the design was to maximize the exterior spaces surrounding the homes in order to create a community bond between the residents of the six separate homes.

←↙↓

Private Space

Each of the six homes have balconies and windows that face inwards towardt the courtyard and outwards to the gardens, offering public and private moments depending on the mood.

↑

Age-Inclusive Design

A variety of indoor and outdoor spaces encourages different forms of interaction between the generations, such as sharing a meal, playing in the courtyard, or tending to the flower and vegetable gardens.

↓

How It All Works

From the street, the complex appears as one sprawling building. Yet the four, three-story houses and two, two-story houses are arranged around a central courtyard on the upper-ground floor.

→

Connections

A communal terrace with chairs and tables on the upper-ground floor connects some of the homes. The layout encourages an intentional community of families to spend time together.

A First Co-housing Community in Cambridge

Project
Marmalade Lane

Designer
Mole Architects

Location
Cambridge, U.K.

Marmalade Lane is a development consisting of 42 homes: a mix of two to five-bedroom terraced houses and apartments, with shared facilities and gardens designed to encourage communal living. This includes a common house with varying functions according to differing weekly needs—there is a playroom, laundry facilities, and a large hall and kitchen for shared group meals and parties. Fostering the group's aim for multinational and intergenerational living, the diverse group includes young families, retired and professional couples, and households of different ages and backgrounds. No matter their size of dwelling, all residents of this micro-neighborhood participate in its administration. Marmalade Lane is Cambridge's first enabled cohousing scheme, and a prime example of the lived in-house sharing experience. "Containing subtle and sophisticated outdoor spaces in every grade for private and public use, the street is where children are able to play under the gentle gaze of parents and neighbors," says the firm.

↓↓

Communal Space

Shared communal areas, such as the courtyards, playroom, and common house, enable socializing and free play, particularly among the younger members of this micro neighborhood.

↑

Connections

Most homes in Marmalade Lane have open backyards that spill out onto a common walkway. Almost identical in design, they present a harmonious and visually cohesive architectural style.

Where Young and Old Come Together

Project

Future Sølund

Designer

C. F. Møller Architects

Location

Copenhagen, Denmark

Future Sølund is a forward-thinking integrated care home program that provides new opportunities for people from all walks of life to interact with one another. Located directly next to the Sortedam Lake in central Copenhagen, the project combines 360 nursing home dwellings, 150 residential units for young people (including 20 for those with disabilities), and shops and cafes facing the lake, all with considered technological solutions for their inhabitants' welfare. The complex is a wonderful example of setting higher standards for aged care, well-being, security, and community values, and demonstrates how young people and the elderly can live inclusively and in harmony; where people in need of care and connection are not marginalized or separated from other people. "Whether the elderly spend most of their time in their homes, or explore the surrounding areas on the site, they will always belong to a larger community," says the firm.

THE BEATLES
LOPPE
MARKED
LØRDAG
OG
SØNDAG
10 15

↖

Communal Space

The main social area, Generation's Square, acts as a meeting place and provides a space for public programs, where residents are encouraged to mingle with each other.

←

Age-Inclusive Design

In general, senior homes are situated on the ground floor, each with their own private front yard. Young families and youth residences are located on higher floors, all with balcony views.

↑

Private Space

Each home is well-lit and can be personalized by each resident. Whether they spend most of their time in the home, or out socializing, they still belong to a larger community.

Neighborly Living

In Europe, intergenerational multifamily homes are creating a sense of community among generations.

In House of Generations in Aarhus, Denmark—a new housing community located in a new harborside urban district—you might share a kitchen and living room with a senior citizen, a student, and a family of four. In shared space running throughout the community's eight buildings you might befriend a disabled neighbor, interact with an elderly neighbor living in one of the nursing homes, or engage with children that are part of the daycare.

"It is a house for a mix of generations. But in this project we are mixing them very much as a melting pot," says architect Claus Jensen, a partner at Copenhagen-based firm RUM who designed the project together with ERIK arkitekter. "Instead of just making one part of the house for elder people and another for the kindergarten, we are actually mixing [them]."

Beyond multigenerational homes shared by the same family, intergenerational living is distinguished here—in Europe—as multifamily homes where entire communities live together. From multiple apartment blocks to several homes under one roof, from cooperative living to collective living to cohousing, these shared living communities prioritize common space as much as private space, extend their reach beyond the community to the neighborhood, and offer the opportunity for the various generations to benefit from one another.

"More and more people want to live in a community beyond the traditional family model," says architect and curator Ilka Ruby in the trailer for *Together! The New Architecture of the Collective*, an exhibition presenting the rising trend in collective building and living.

This "silent revolution in contemporary architecture" as she and co-curator Andreas Ruby call it, is a response to housing scarcity →

"I think we're going to see lots of projects like the House of Generations in other places, in Denmark and the rest of the world."

Previous Page
A housing cooperative on the Spree River in Berlin, Spreefeld opens itself to the neighborhood.

Top Left
Among its 64 apartments, the Spreefeld complex includes 6 cluster apartments' where residents share a kitchen and a living room.

Bottom Left
Community space on the ground floor can be reserved by non-residents.

and unaffordability and social shifts in household makeup. "For many, collective living is a vision that promises to counteract loneliness while keeping prices affordable," they note.

Communal living is a way of life that dates back hundreds of years. In fact, the cohousing trend has been likened to the way people lived in medieval Europe, where households of not just relatives but strangers was the norm. It wasn't until the industrial age in the later half of the nineteenth century that families separated into smaller units and households shrunk. But, as has been the case historically, new models of living emerged in response.

According to a paper written by *Kollektivus*, Sweden's national cohousing association, "in different periods various models for more neighborly housing with shared services have been launched. These models [were] motivated sometimes as social and political visions and sometimes as practical solutions to the needs of day-to-day life." The paper states that the brutal changes that industrialization brought in Europe provoked visions of an egalitarian society and where working and living were collectively organized. An early example was Frenchman Charles Fourier's *Phalanstère*, a utopian living concept uniting workers of various social classes under one Palace of Versailles-like complex, joining residential with collective space. From there the concept spread throughout Europe, followed by the housing cooperatives of the 1920s, the hippie communes in the sixties, and the origins of modern coliving in Denmark in the 1970s. Like the rise of the sharing economy, new typologies emerge that speak to the particular times and aim to meet that need.

An example of this is at the House of Generations, with its cluster apartments, which sit alongside residences for elders and people with disabilities, family homes, and dedicated apartments for young people. Here, these smaller apartments sit within a larger cluster and all use shared space, each with access to a shared kitchen and living room. "Some of [the clusters] are just for young people and some are only for elderly people, but most of them are mixed," says Jensen. "So people are living very close to each other with different generations." →

Top Right
House of Generations in Aarhus, Denmark, encourages its residents to mix together.

Bottom Right
House of Generations offers two types of housing typologies, with different levels of privacy and common space.

Residents can choose their desired level of community through the house's two housing typologies: the neighborhood or the housing community. Those who choose the latter opt to share common space, while residents in the former choose slightly larger apartments (and more privacy) as the common space is eliminated. But they can benefit from the common space throughout the development, including rooftop gardens, workshops, multipurpose halls, large kitchens, a library, fitness, and wellness areas and a restaurant open to the public. "It's almost like a cruise," Jensen says, speaking to the community's roughly 27,000-square-meters, as well as the variety of its shared offerings. Apartment sizes vary but all are kept smaller to encourage residents to come together in the common space.

"The idea is to actually cut a big part of these square meters and put the residents in the common activities and [common] areas," Jensen says.

Common space and the cluster apartment are also integral components of Spreefeld, a riverside housing cooperative on the Spree River in Berlin, Germany. Comprising three buildings and a population that is described as multigenerational and multicultural, the cooperative includes 64 apartments that range in size from 270-square-feet (25-square-meters) up to the largest of six cluster apartments at 7,590-square-feet (705-square-meters).

"The question was more how could you make a structure that would allow as many typologies as possible," says architect Florian Köhl of Berlin-based firm Fatkoehl Architekten. "How could you make a building that would become architecture and at the same time would allow this kind of flexibility." Together with Carpaneto Schöningh Architekten and BARarchitekten, Fatkoehl designed the buildings—working closely with the cooperative. In the building Köhl and his team focused on, a one-and-half-floor cluster apartment includes a shared kitchen, living room, and terrace, along with a communal bathroom and a guest-room. Each of the cluster's residents has their own private space with a bedroom, bathroom, and kitchenette.

Along with shared rooftop terraces, fitness rooms, and guest rooms, the community's ground floor includes workshop space, a large kitchen, coworking space, a daycare, and so-called option space, which can be reserved by non-residents. The ground floor space is largely open to the public as one of the major goals of the project was to keep the public space as unrestricted as possible to allow access to the river. The positioning of the buildings forms an open courtyard, creating a pathway to the river.

"The architecture engages with the surroundings, with the city, as a sort of physical grown thing, but also with the people," Köhl says. "And then you have these vertical gardens, [the balconies], that allow you to be both inside and outside at the same time, but also they allow people that come to see this kind of exhibition of gardens." →

Left
Future Sølund by C. F. Møller Architects and Tredje Natur is one of the largest and most visionary residential and care home projects in Danish history.

Bottom Left
Marmalade Lane is Cambridge, UK's first enabled cohousing community.

Below
The diverse blend of residents of Marmalade Lane share common space including a common house.

In Almere, Netherlands, Oosterwold Coliving Complex is its own unique typology. Nine 1,722-square-feet (160-square meter) apartments are set side by side in one 1,080-foot-long (100-meter-long) structure. Designed by Mathijs Cremers of ZakenMaker and Bureau SLA, the project was initiated by Dutch artist Frode Bolhuis who desired a live/work lifestyle with lots of green space. Working with an extremely tight budget, he invited eight friends to join him.

"We made this super simple idea," says Cremers of the project, which, along with its length, stands out for its seamless glass facades and floating appearance as it is raised slightly above the ground. "We have a thick floor and a thick roof, and everything in between is up to them." While some, like Bolhuis, have incorporated a workspace, others have kept their home entirely living space while others included small spaces to accommodate aging parents in the future. "If you see these dwellings next to each other, they're all super different on the inside," Cremers says.

Together, the group shares a collective garden and a deck that runs continuously around the long home. "You open up one door and you see these children running about the entire building. And people yelling, 'Is my kid at your place?', 'Yes!'," Cremers says. "It's super simple, but it works really well." A second house, mirroring the first exactly, followed immediately after. A third was on the way.

Future Sølund, located in Copenhagen's Nørrebro district and designed by C. F. Møller Architects in collaboration with Tredje Natur, is yet another example. A pioneering care center integrated into the city, the close to 430,500-square-foot (40,000-square-meter) residence includes 360 care homes, 150 youth homes, 20 senior dwellings, and a daycare center. The building is centered around a large semi-public square and two smaller private squares, with ground floor common space including workshops, cafes, rehabilitation centers, and shops.

Like all of the communities, it has the potential to make once strangers of various generations feel like family. "You are able to have some kind of a new family," Jensen says. "You are able to find a grandmother as your neighbor." •

Celebrating Communal Living

Project

3 generation house

Designer

BETA office for architecture and the city

Location

Amsterdam, Netherlands

This five-story tower, designed for three generations of a Dutch family, is an example of how multigenerational living benefits city dwellers of all ages. Two separate apartments are stacked directly above one another to create a home where the family and their elderly parents can enjoy each other's company without sacrificing the advantages of privacy. Unlike many multistory homes, the elderly couple live on the top-floor apartment which has been accessibly designed to accommodate wheelchairs and reduced physical ability. When needed, the entire building can be reconfigured into four apartments, allowing the children to have their own space once they grow up. The sculptural home features a lot of concrete, with bright yellow painted walls providing the interior spaces with vibrant pops of color. The home is a great example of cohabiting in an urban context, and a reminder that all generations should look out for one another.

↑ Communal Space
Structural concrete walls define the form of the interior spaces, but the architects wanted to add some vibrancy to the home. An angular staircase is painted bright yellow to make a visual impact.

↓

Private Space

Light partition walls separate the rooms into two areas. The whole building is designed so it can be reconfigured from two apartments into four, accommodating changing demands over time.

←

Private Space

The building does not have one specific communal space for group encounters. Both apartments within the structure have large living spaces and balconies with views of Amsterdam.

↑

Connections

The dining area features a single-wall kitchen, warm timber, and a long wooden dining table. This zone shows how multiple parts of the home are joined by the sculptural staircase.

→

Age-Inclusive Design

The grandparents live in the topmost apartment, which has an elevator, level floors, and wider door openings for accessibility in old age. Also included is a large terrace where other family members can come to relax.

A Garage, Reimagined for Granny

Project
Granny Pad

Designer
Best Practice

Location
Seattle, WA, USA

What was formerly an unused garage in the backyard of a family property has been transformed into a sleek home for the client's grandmother. The structure is entirely separated from the main house, providing her privacy and independence whenever she desires it. With its simple typology consisting of two connecting volumes with pitched roofs, Granny Pad's conversion provides the family with a cost-effective solution to the lack of housing for their loved one. Clad in black-stained cedar wood panels, the exterior is dark and moody, offset by a door painted in a bright pink hue. Double-height ceilings in the space make the modest footprint of the Granny Pad feel lofty and spacious, while the light plywood interior and skylights fill the dwelling with natural light. With this design, the architects have imagined an adaptable space that could, over time, be used as a home office or studio, or as a revenue stream to rent out to tenants, or simply move in themselves as empty nesters.

↑ → **Flexible Design**
Converted from a garage, the space can be used for current and future needs. It can be a home office or studio in the years to come, a rental property, or a space for the parents as empty nesters.

↖↑→

Communal Space
Currently, the grandmother lives in the space alone, yet her open-plan home has space for her children and grandchildren to visit, cook meals, or work on the vegetable patch together.

←

Age-Inclusive Design
Due to the decreased mobility associated with age, the grand-mother's living areas all needed to be on one level. A tiled pathway alongside the garden connects back to the main house.

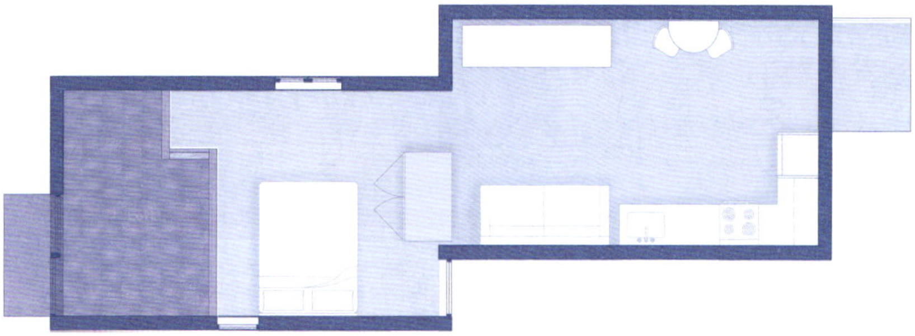

Granny Pad Loft Level Plan

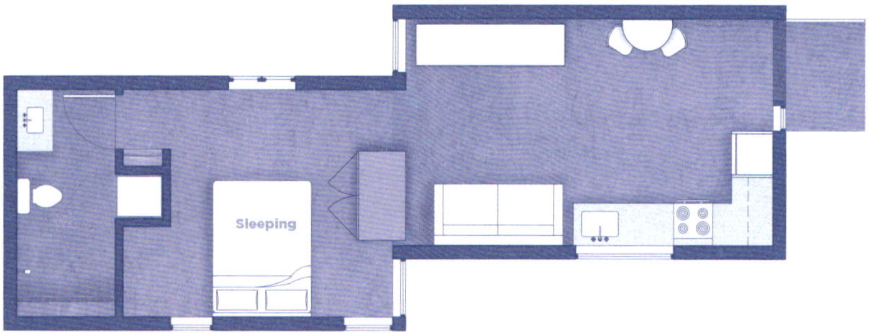

Granny Pad Main Level Plan

←

Connections

The project is a great solution for the family who were struggling to find affordable housing for their grandmother. Now, she lives in a contemporary, safe, and cozy home close to her relatives.

→

Private Space

A lofted space above the bathroom, accessible via a ladder, is used for storage for now. Should the parents decide to transform the space in the future, it can be used as a studio or office.

A Home Bridging Nature and Tradition

Project
Choy House

Designer
O'Neill Rose Architects

Location
New York, NY, USA

The borough of Queens in New York City is architecturally defined by single family homes. With this in mind, the firm's challenge was to design three homes under one roof, while keeping in line with the visual appearance of neighboring properties. Choy House aims to redefine the idea of the American home by combining Chinese traditions of living with extended family members with the nuclear family set-up that is common to American home ownership. Finding a balance between these two notions, the home caters to a couple, their two small children, his younger brother and wife, and their mother, who is the matriarch of the family. The client, also a builder, was involved in the home's conception, placing importance on repurposing excess materials throughout the space. The ground floor, designed with floor-to-ceiling windows, is where the grandmother lives. Readily accessible, an exterior stepped garden grows herbs and vegetables used for home cooking and it is also an ideal space to watch her grandchildren play.

← ↖ ↑

Communal Space
The stepped garden, filled with plants, flowers, and herbs, is visible through the ceiling-height windows. Contemporary furnishings with colored accents create bright and welcoming spaces.

↘

How It All Works

Three separate homes exist on the property: the grandmother's on the lower-ground floor and two, two-story homes directly above for the two brothers and their families.

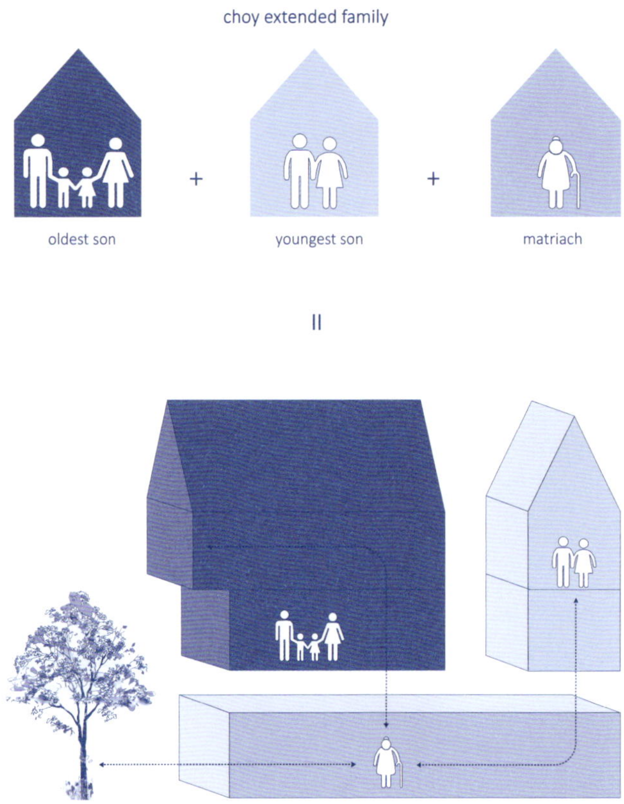

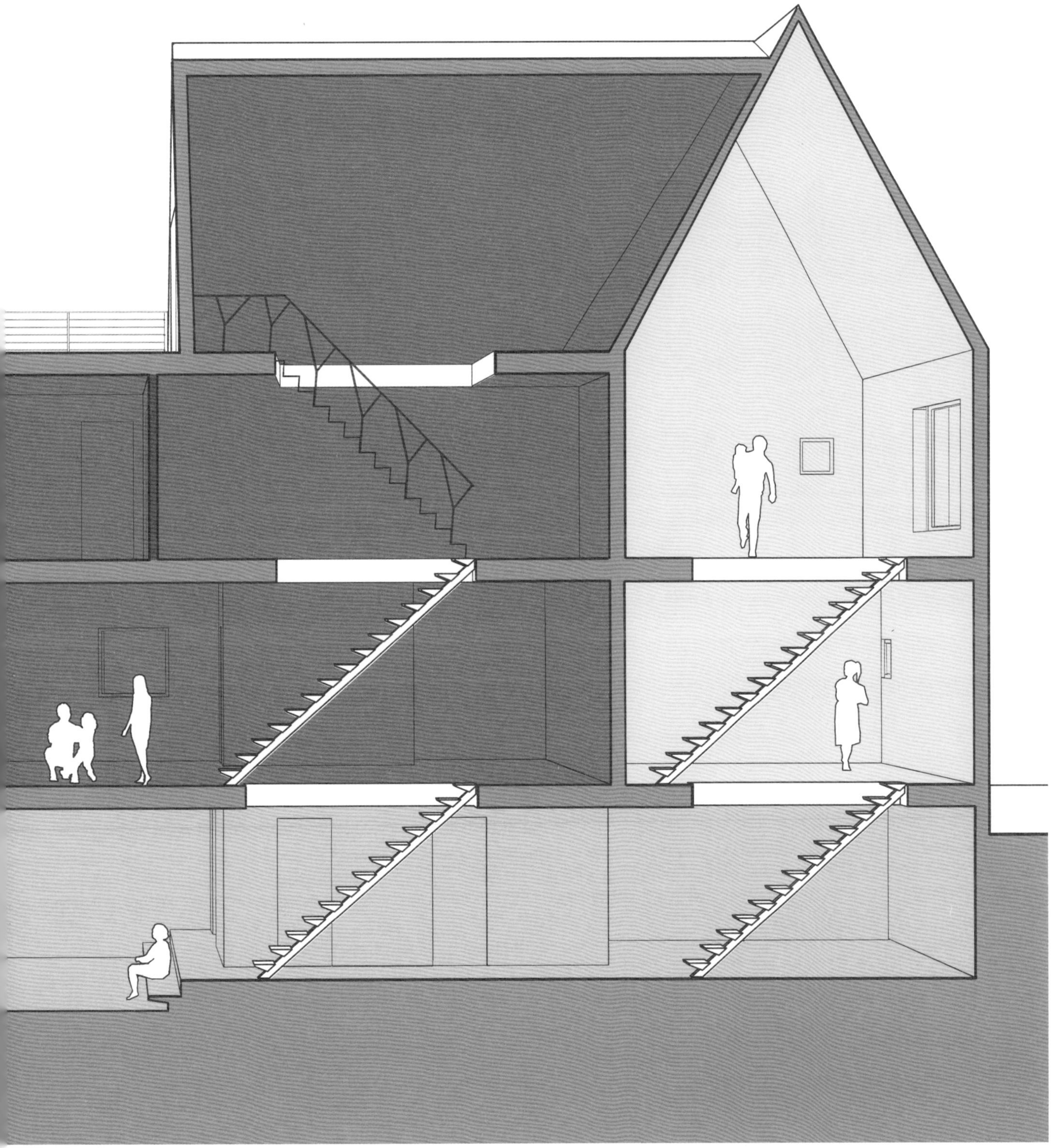

DESIGNED FOR CHANGE

Flexibility is at the heart of this easily adaptable, extended family home that values ecological, economic, and cultural sustainability.

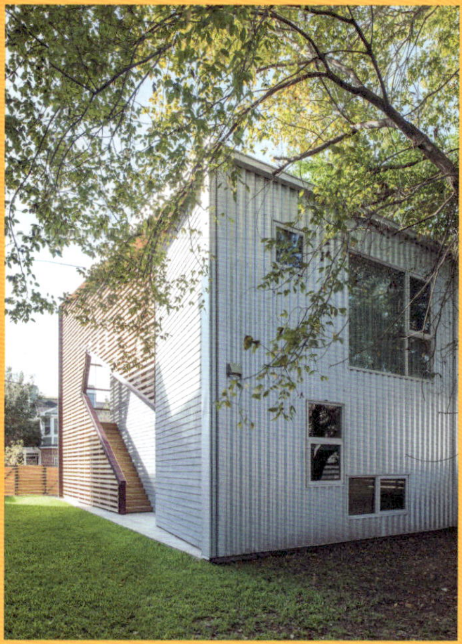

The beauty of Shotgun Chameleon, according to the architect Zui Ng of Houston-based ZDES, is that you don't have to do anything. It can easily adapt to support a single family home, a home for extended family, or parts of it can be rented out to generate income. All you need to do is close the door to the interior stairs. "You open it up, it's a three-bedroom," Ng says. "You close it, it's a duplex."

Along with his wife and their young daughter, Ng has called Shotgun Chameleon home for more than six years. The trio share this adaptable, two-level home with his parents, who are now in their seventies. This is their second time living in the Shotgun Chameleon with Ng, having moved in earlier to care for their granddaughter.

The project, designed to easily transition with the family, dates back to Ng's undergraduate years. The then-architecture student conceived it as a housing prototype for a competition held in response to rebuilding New Orleans following Hurricane Katrina. With the idea to create a home that could adapt to its particular context, the flexible residence was inspired by the vernacular shotgun house, a modest housing type found in the southern part of the United States, where, in addition to the linear layout offering a clear path for natural ventilation, the front part of the home, which also has a backdoor, was often rented out to generate income.

"I thought I should do something similar," says Ng. His contemporary interpretation easily converts a three-bedroom home into an upper and lower duplex. "So the bottom can be used for anything you want. You can give it to your parents to live in, you can use it as a store, or as a rental for income. It's very flexible."

Distinguished by a geometric cutout on its east side, the boxy, breezy home is located in Houston's Fourth Ward, a historic African American neighbourhood where a number of older shotgun houses still remain. "This neighborhood just called for [the project]," Ng says. "It was like a perfect match."

With a balcony on its upper level and porch on its ground level, the south-facing home is clad in perforated stainless steel on its street-facing side and slated pine wood—inspired by fences—on its sides, both allowing in light and gentle wind. The latter also acts as a porous means of privacy for Ng and his neighbors. Behind the cutout, an exterior set of stairs offers a private entrance to Ng's family's upper level residence via the balcony where family and friends gather. Here, tall ceilings and the perforated metal were precisely designed to bring in abundant sunlight in winter and less in summer, to warm the house and keep it cool, respectively, in concert with passive ventilation. Large sliding doors open into the upper level, an open-plan living room/dining room/kitchen, made spacious through continued high ceilings and a tall transom window above the sliders framing an ever-changing urban landscape.

Clad in a palette of plywood—stained by Ng in its entirety—the home's two levels essentially mirror one another with living space →

Previous Pages
A door to the interior stairs allows this home to easily morph from a single family home to a duplex and on to other uses.

The design is inspired by the shotgun house, a common style in the region.

Left
The home sustains the neighborhood culture through elements like balconies on the upper floor and a porch on its ground level.

Right
Pinewood slatting, inspired by fences, brings in a breeze and helps maintain privacy between neighbors.

Left
Thanks to its precise design, the house keeps the sun out in summer but brings it in during the winter.

placed in the front, street-facing side, and retreat-like bedrooms in the back with tranquil views to the garden. However, the ground-floor living space, reached through its private porch entrance, can be converted into a third bedroom. Its kitchenette is tucked into a corner in the corridor just outside the back bedroom's bathroom.

With bookshelves on the staircase-facing side and a flat side to make it seamlessly disappear on the side facing the ground floor, a door cleverly splits the house into two. Along with their own kitchens, bathrooms, and outdoor spaces, the levels also invite privacy through separate entrances. A third entrance at the bottom of the exterior stairs to the ground level offers a place for the generations to gather on benches in the calm, tree-filled back garden.

Along with the home's adaptability, its approach to sustainability distinguishes the design. "Sustainability in terms of ecology, economy, and culture," says Ng. Using the ground level as a rental unit in between his parent's living there, Ng was able to pay off the house through the generated income. "This house can actually pay for itself," he says. From a cultural perspective, the house takes a chameleon-like approach. Ng explains, "so it's trying to mimic and blend in with the culture." It honors the materials of its immediate surroundings and reinterprets them. It attempts to sustain the neighborhood culture by incorporating vernacular elements like the balcony and porch used to create a connection with the neighbors and the view.

"Every single view has its own purpose," Ng says of the home's various windows. His mother takes advantage of a low ground-floor window meant for prayer. His father recently took over another lower ground-floor window in the bedroom that, during their first time living in the home, his mother enjoyed her meals while looking out at the garden. Along with the idea that the flexible home could offer Ng's parents a place to comfortably age in place, the architect thought even further. "I actually thought beyond that, I thought, I'm going to live downstairs when I'm old," he says. "I only have one daughter, and if she chooses to live with me, she's welcome, and she can use the upstairs and me and my wife can live downstairs comfortably." •

"You open it up, it's a three-bedroom. You close it, it's a duplex."

A Family Affair in San Francisco

Project

Terrace House

Designer

Aidlin Darling Design

Location

San Francisco, CA, USA

This vertical, three-story modern home captivates with its floor-to-ceiling glass windows that provide iconic views of the city. Located in the hilly neighborhood of Castro Heights, the sculpted home is capped by a flat roof adorned with a green garden. The clients—two grandparents, two parents, and their three sons—wanted a highly crafted yet energy-efficient home that would prioritize biophilic elements. "Natural materials are integrated at each level within the interior, and occupants are provided with direct visual and physical access to nature," the firm explains. The ground floor, where the grandparents' and childrens' bedrooms are, opens onto a terraced backyard garden, and is designed to foster bonding between the younger and elder family members. On the second floor, all three generations gather to eat, work, or relax around the shared kitchen, dining, and living rooms, complete with a cozy fireplace and intimate nooks.

↑ **Communal Space**
The home has floor-to-ceiling glass walls on the east and west facades, allowing direct sunlight into the whole interior in the morning and evening. A contemporary fireplace provides a cozy environment for gathering.

↑

Connections

The design-conscious family have many statement pieces and sculptures around the home. Next to the staircase, within a three-story mahogany cabinet there is a hidden powder room, study, and closet.

→

Private Space

Intimate nooks can be found all around the home. The master suite, with its built-in window daybed, provides the couple with a calm, scenic retreat away from the children's liveliness.

Two Generations by the Creek

Project
House on Ancaster Creek

Designer
Williamson Williamson

Location
Ancaster, Canada

This modern L-shaped home, House on Ancaster Creek, charmingly named for its location near a protected watercourse, was informed by the clients' need for a living experience that could be practical, contemporary, and comfortable. Responding to this brief, the firm aimed to navigate the complexity of multigenerational living, so that the owners and their elderly parents could all inhabit the home with room to spare. Varied living spaces with views of the creek are set along the main volume, which enables the landscape to appear as if meandering through the house. On the ground floor, the grandparents' suite contains a kitchenette with its own seating area, bedroom, and bathroom, alongside the main kitchen, living, and dining rooms. The project confirms that "sustainable systems and designing for the elderly are not exclusive from modern expression and exquisite details." The firm has demonstrated that well-designed housing can embrace new ways of traditional living: as the family changes, so can the family home.

↑ → **Flexible Design**
Social areas converge around a courtyard with a tree. The large home has an additional bedroom intended to be used by guests or a live-in caretaker, depending on the family's changing needs.

↓

Communal Space
Positioning the main living areas in the center of the home allows them to be shared by both generations, and include ceiling-height windows that overlook the landscape.

→

Connections
A spiralling wooden staircase adds an interesting geometry and contributes to the home's contemporary aesthetic. It leads upstairs to the younger home-owner's sleeping quarters and home offices.

A Home Nods to its Rural Surrounding

Project

Whidbey Farm

Designer

MW Works

Location

Whidbey Island, WA, USA

The owners of this contemporary home, a senior couple with ties to the land going back several generations, wanted to build a new home on the site of their farm property that could accommodate their three adult children and multiple grandchildren, hosting up to 20 people in total. Whidbey Farm is a modern country home that overlooks the forest on one side and a mossy pond and meadow with chicken sheds and grazing cattle on the other. The owners wanted the trees to remain protected as possible, so the home's design works its way around the forest, with specially engineered foundations for the stone walls that dodge important tree roots in the ground. Both warm and rustic, the home embodies a stylish aesthetic and is designed for low-maintenance longevity as the couple live out their years there. Floor-to-ceiling glass walls frame exterior views of the stunning scenery. This home is perfectly suited for summer barbecues, holiday gatherings, water sports, and fishing.

↓ → →

Communal Space

The contemporary home overlooks a mossy pond and meadow, and includes spacious living areas to relax in. An earthy color palette with a stone fireplace adds to the warm and rustic atmosphere.

←

Private Space

A separate living quarter exists as a guest dwelling above the garage, complete with a bedroom, and a separate area to relax with views of the surrounding native greenery.

↓ →

Private Space
The different volumes are linked visually and physically by a courtyard that provides access and connection to one another, but still allows for separation and retreat when desired.

↓

How It All Works

The three volumes converge around a central courtyard of trees and plant life, all of which are oriented in different directions to maximize the views. Overall, the house is designed for longevity.

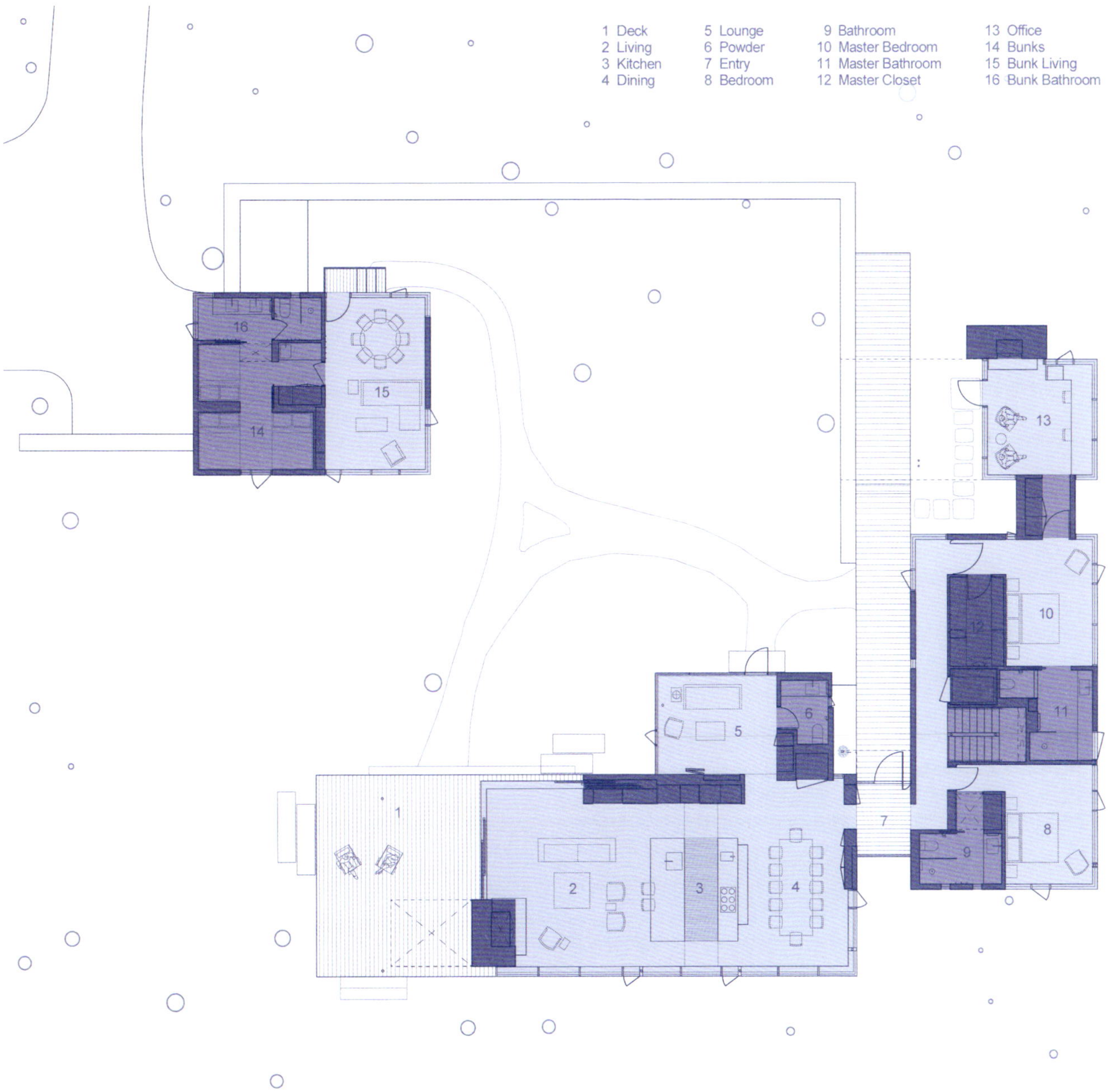

How To Design for Multiple Generations

Flexible spaces, age-inclusive design, and communal spaces are just a few of the different ways that multigenerational homes must accommodate their ever-changing residents.

Designing a home for multiple generations goes far beyond just designing a residence for a big family, or just designing a big home. It's more than just moving in the in-laws when they've grown older, or an adult son or daughter just moving back into their childhood bedroom. A multigenerational home is purpose-built and designed to accommodate the needs and considerations of the various generations from grandparents to adult children to grandkids—and how they all live together.

Toronto-based practice Williamson Williamson is intimately familiar with the concerns of families who have decided to share a multi-generational home. "They didn't want it to feel like they were back in high school, and living in their parents' basement," says principal Betsy Williamson, referring to House on Ancaster Creek and Grange Triple Double, two among the number of multigenerational homes the firm has designed in Canada. Both were commissioned by the families' younger generation to share with their parents. "They didn't want to have the roles reversed back to their childhood, but wanted to find a way they could be a mature family and have parents with them at the same time."

How do adult children live with their parents? And how do their parents live with them? How do both generations share a space but →

"You don't have to custom design your own home and be able to afford that to be able to take some of the ideas that we're putting together and use them in your own way."

Previous Page
Architect Ryan Bollom designed Dakota Mountain as a multi-generational home for his family in Texas Hill Country.

Top Left
Dakota Mountain balances the private space with space to connect.

Bottom Left
A shared pantry is the connecting piece between the two sides of this two-in-one multigenerational design.

maintain their independence? These are among the concerns when designing for a multigenerational family. So too is adapting spaces for seniors, without making them feel old or ostracized and their spaces feel sterile. As is designing a flexible home that can grow and change with the family: to create a home that can carry on through the generations and beyond.

Working with the constraints and advantages of the particular site, personal wishes, and other considerations, architects are balancing proximity alongside privacy, incorporating age-inclusive design that doesn't feel aged, and flexibility for both today and tomorrow to design extended family homes that are livable from one generation to the next.

Located in Hamilton, Ontario, Williamson Williamson's House on Ancaster Creek stacks two volumes on top of one another perpendicularly. At their corner meeting point, the lower level houses a self-contained apartment for the elderly in-laws and the upper level a private master suite. "[The clients requested] the master suite really be somewhere where they felt that when they went there it was their own private sanctuary," Williamson says. "Thus the big, kind of exuberant staircase; they really wanted to feel like they were kind of going somewhere when they went upstairs."

Including a courtyard space that pushes back into the dining room and extends onto a deck, the home also needed to accommodate the owner's mother who suffered from Alzheimer's disease. Along with well-lit spaces for "aging eyes," Williamson says, the accessible apartment includes thoughtfully placed drains in case water is left on, an induction cooktop, and a master switch in the shared laundry room that allows the younger couple to discretely shut off their parents' section in the evening without having to disturb. "It's again a question of making it so [the younger couple] can have autonomy and they don't have to be checking in all the time," Williamson says. Here a bedroom with a bathroom down the hall could accommodate a live-in caregiver. At another property, Grange Triple Double, the inclusion of a ground floor apartment opens up a variety of possibilities. "The big idea is about treating living →

Right
Flexibility is key in multigen design. This granny flat has been designed to easily transition to other uses and users.

Bottom Right
Dignified design, for aging in one place, makes a home feel like a home—and not a hospital.

Bottom Left
A sweeping staircase offers a definitive transition from shared space to private sanctuary.

Below
The Dakota Mountain residence combines communal spaces, such as shared powder room and outdoor space, with private spaces such as a primary and secondary kitchen.

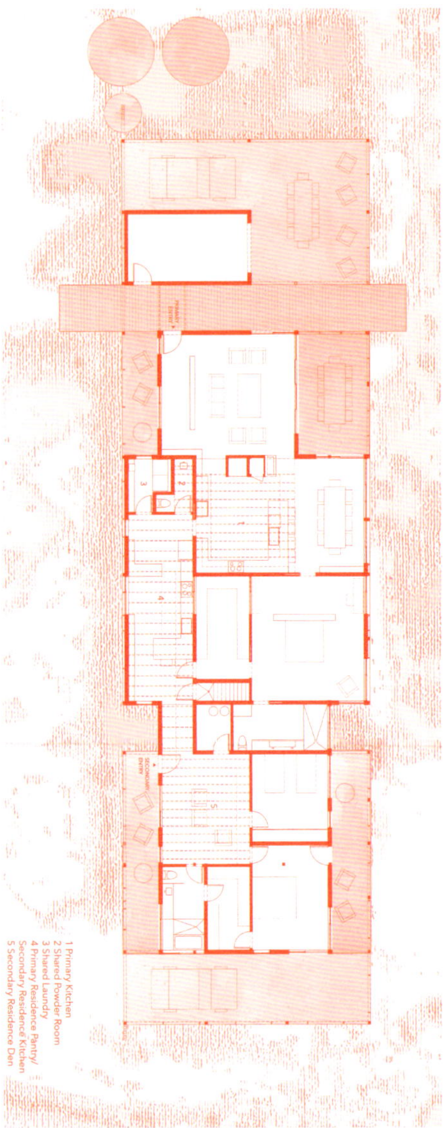

considerations for older people more like a home that has been modified as opposed to the hospitalization model, where you go to a nursing home and it's like being in a hospital that kind of looks like a house," Williamson says. "It's about [coming] from the other direction."

On a tight urban lot in Toronto, Grange Triple Double includes a private deck off the upper level master bedroom, a private terrace off a second floor suite equipped with a kitchenette, and on the ground level, where a separate apartment can be connected or separated from the main house, a spacious patio for the entire family. Separate outdoor spaces as well as separate entrances allow for privacy, while the ground floor apartment can not only function as an accessible self-contained space for the grandparents with a direct connection to their family in the main home, but it can also extend into the basement apartment to create a larger apartment; or the two spaces can be used separately. "How can the spaces change and how can you use them differently over time?" Williamson says. So far, because the grandparents decided to occupy the coveted upper level master suite for the time being, the husband has housed his business in the basement and rented out the ground floor apartment space to outside tenants.

"We called Grange Triple Double a prototype because we wanted people to copy it. If you can take these ideas and use them on your own, we really encourage that," Williamson says. "You don't have to custom design your own home and be able to afford that to be able to take some of the ideas that we're putting together and use them in your own way."

Through the very personal experience of designing his own multi-generational home—shared with his wife, two children, and his in-laws, architect Auguste van Oppen, of Amsterdam-based BETA architects also understands that just because families have made the decision to live together, it certainly doesn't mean they want to be together all the time. "That's probably the biggest challenge," says van Oppen, "to design proximity but also to make sure these two worlds can live next to each other without an invasion of their personal sphere." In his case, privacy is achieved by designing two or more independent but interdependent homes within one. This setup—two apartments stacked one on top of another inside one five-story home—offers the space to retreat, as well as the option for each generation to remain in their respective spaces.

As exemplified in the home, the key is making the spaces senior-friendly but not feel senior, by subtly incorporating the necessary elements into the design and by making them a natural part of the family home. Architects like van Oppen focus on accessibility as a core requirement first and foremost by designing level floors and wider doorways to easily allow for wheelchairs and walkers. Many apartments and spaces for grandparents are on the ground floor or, if on the upper level, as is the case with the 3 Generation House in Amsterdam, an elevator can be incorporated to facilitate movement. →

Left
In this vertical two-in-one multigen design, two apartments are stacked one on top of the other.

But multigenerational homes can also be designed to easily shape-shift for the future through simple construction adjustments. The second floor space in van Oppen's house, currently used as guestrooms for his in-law's apartment, can easily be allocated to his family's lower level apartment to create a larger space for them. In addition, two studio apartments—with the possibility of future use for his children when they are older—can be created through reconfiguring the levels on the north facade, transforming the home from two dwellings to four. "In an ideal situation you would not have surplus space in your household," says van Oppen.

While van Oppen's home stretches vertically, many two-in-one multigenerational homes are integrated into one long horizontal line, with the two generation's homes on each end, connected together by a central breezeway, an entryway, or shared space. Inside Dakota Mountain, a multigenerational home designed by Austin, Texas-based architect Ryan Bollom of Low Design Office (LOWDO), the connecting piece is a shared pantry. "My mother loves to cook for the whole family," says Bollom. A clever cut through from the master bedroom's closet to the pantry allows his mother a quick connection to family in the other home.

Privacy and connection are also achieved through outdoor space. Dakota Mountain includes decks and porches on both ends of the home, as well as tucked into spaces on the sides.

The entire home, including the secondary residence, was made wheelchair accessible. This allows family members to adapt as needed. When they're older, Bollom's parents could downsize into the smaller space, and a member from the younger generation could move into the other side to manage the larger home and take care of them. The idea is about designing flexible homes that can evolve with the family: homes that can accommodate shifting needs, shrink and grow, expand and contract to serve changing spatial demands and multiple functions even beyond the family.

In his own family home, Bollom addresses this larger idea. "It's not going to stop with them," he says. "It's meant to really function in multiple ways, beyond just our family and accommodate whatever the user's needs are, and hopefully be flexible enough to do that." •

A Stacked Home on a Corner Lot

Project
Grange Triple Double

Designer
Williamson Williamson

Location
Toronto, Canada

A corner site in Toronto's Chinatown provides a lively and spacious context for Grange Triple Double, a bright multiunit home that blends the needs of two households into one: a professional couple with a young son, and two empty nester grandparents. Together, they've created an ideal scenario for living that allows for full autonomy and close connection at the same time. The family have cleverly maximized the built form of the home: spatially, the property consists of a single family home stacked on top of the grandparents' suite, which in turn is stacked on top of a ground floor and basement apartment, which is at times rented out to other tenants. The extended family share the ground floor courtyard that connects to the living spaces, while terraces on each level provide private spaces for everyone to enjoy. Recycled white-painted bricks and red cedar panels compose the building's facade, which appears like a LEGO block from the street.

↑ → Communal Space
The grandparents love looking after their young grandchild and often get together on their private terrace. Right: The home's stepped exterior reaches the maximum height permitted by the city's zoning plans.

↑
Communal Space
With sliding glass doors, the bright kitchen spills out onto the terrace, blurring indoor and outdoor living. Contrasting materials of different types of wood were chosen for warmth and durability.

←
Flexible Design
In the future, the family plans to use the house and apartments in different ways. When the children are grown up, they can move into a rental unit, while the parents may move into the ground floor apartment.

→

Age-Inclusive Design

The grandparents and couple each have private and protected terraces. If needed, the aging grandparents can live in a small apartment that is connected to the shared family spaces.

↓

How It All Works

The multiuse dwelling consists of separate living spaces stacked on top of one another: a basement rental unit, a ground-floor home for the family with a courtyard to share, and a suite for the grandparents.

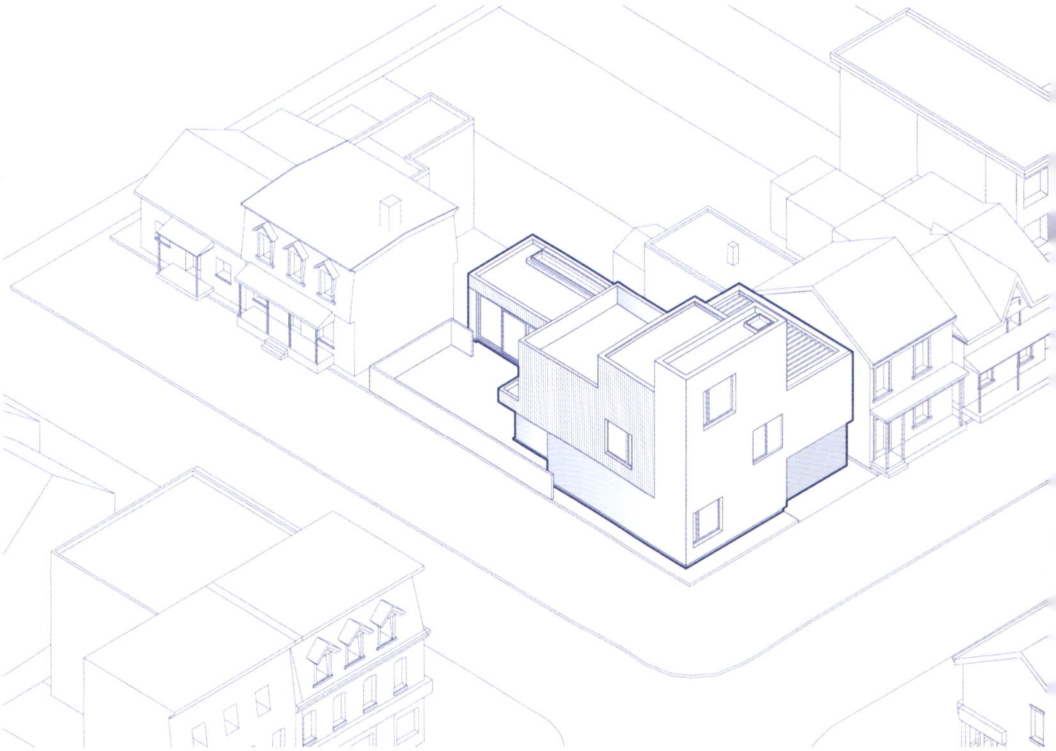

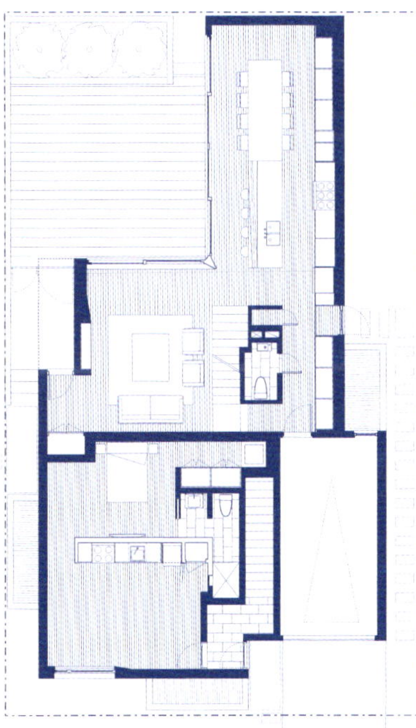

A Spacious House For The Summer

Project
Summerhouse

Designer
Maka Arkitektur

Location
Torekov, Sweden

Once an old fishing village, the town of Torekov, in the southernmost province of Sweden, is one of the country's most loved holiday destinations. Here, a family of three generations approached Maka Arkitektur to design a holiday house for them to use in the summer months. The generously-sized home, designed to accommodate up to 12 people, makes use of the site by wrapping itself around a central courtyard. Its volumes consist of a main building and two wings, one of which is detached as a guest annex with its own kitchenette and bathroom. "The garden is the central space for the family to come together," the firm explains, whereby most of the rooms are arranged around a grassed lawn and a cherry tree. A second smaller courtyard is intended for growing vegetables and to house berry bushes planted by the grandchildren. In order to glimpse views of the nearby ocean, the firm designed a rooftop terrace, contributing to the summerhouse's holiday feel.

↑ Connections
The main rectilinear volume features three bedrooms along with the living and kitchen areas. It connects the two wings on either side, all of which converge around a tranquil garden with a cherry tree.

← ← ↓

Communal Space

Although the site is modestly sized, the architects aimed to create a home with an array of spaces that offer different experiences and degrees of privacy, yet always with a visual connection to the outside.

ONNIERS VEGETARISKA KOKBOK

←

Natural Materials

The material palette is kept simple with long-lasting wooden furnishings and solid oakwood floors throughout the house that will age well.

↑

Age-Inclusive Design

With its pared down kitchen and dining area, the home exudes a sense of calm. Access to everything is made easy for the grandparents, an important consideration that was part of the initial design plan.

A Modern Madrid Villa

Project
Villa Teruca

Designer
EME157

Location
Madrid, Spain

Villa Teruca, an imposing red brick dwelling, is a two-home structure designed for a mother, her son, and her son's young family. The brick facade was chosen as a visual reminder of the mother's previous house, which she lived in for the entirety of her life until moving. From the outside, the large, rectilinear volume appears as one household; yet beneath its walls lie two semi-detached homes side by side, both taking up each floor, with shared access and a garage. "The common spaces are used as meeting and unwinding places, which complement the rest of the house and leave time for family moments," the architects explain. The rooftop terrace celebrates its structural elements as they are, with the polished concrete floor, black metal beams, and punctual holes in the load-bearing brick walls left as finishes. A swimming pool and decking area provide great views over the tree-lined neighborhood, while the interior, pared down and at times industrial-looking, allows sunlight to pour in through large south-facing windows.

↑ → Communal Space
The clean and modern living room is where the residents unwind. Right: The modernist brick facade was chosen as a visual tribute to the mother's previous house.

←

Connections

A swimming pool and decking area is located on the roof-top, providing great outdoor living and views over the neighborhood.

↓

Communal Space

Inside the building, two separate semi-detached homes feature similar interiors, including a modern kitchen, dining spaces, and bookshelves.

↑

Private Space
Contemporary furnishings, artworks, and white walls create bright and welcoming spaces for family moments in both the private and communal areas.

THE CYCLE OF LIFE

A flexible home in Vancouver adapts to meet a multigenerational family's changing needs, today, and into the future.

Located in Vancouver, Canada, this cedar-clad home with a courtyard cut through the center was designed to not only accommodate multiple generations now, but through the various stages of their lives. Inspired by lead interior designer Gail Guevara's personal quest to create a house that allows families to live healthy at home for as long as possible. Full House was conceived through a consideration of potential scenarios spanning 120 years into the future, the three-level home—designed to easily change into three different configurations—allows the various generations to cycle through different areas of the home according to their current stage of life.

"The majority of housing [in Vancouver] seems to be developed only with resale in mind, rather than the idea of growing old in a home and housing a family for 60, 75, 100, even 150 years," says architect Michael Leckie, founder of Leckie Studio Architecture + Design, which designed the 3,505-square-foot (325-square-meter) home. "When you start to think about architecture at that scale, you think about a house differently."

Surrounded by a screen of dark-stained cedar battens, the home—including a laneway house in the backyard which could easily transform into an additional living suite or a caretaker's unit—was commissioned by a young couple who were anticipating starting a family. Gifted the land by the husband's parents with the agreement that the older generation would eventually live and age there, the situation offered a solution to exorbitant land prices and scarcity, and expense of both childcare and elderly care.

Looking through the lens of privacy and connection needs for each current generation and future ones to come, the firm ran through various scenarios that could impact the home over the next century. "What [we were] really doing was identifying the specific [privacy and public connection] requirements of each generation at every stage of life and then sort of suggesting that these are the areas of the house that they're inhabiting through those years," Leckie says.

In its default mode, the house is a five-bedroom home with three bedrooms on its upper level, one bedroom on the ground floor level and the fifth on the lower level. The main floor has a long line of living space—the main connection point between the generations—that flows into outdoor space. It's here on the main level where the architects conceived the idea of a flexible partition inspired by Duchamp's *Door, 11, rue Larrey* in Paris, France. The door—which is currently replaced with a temporary wall as the owners are currently renting out the lower level—can move between three different positions, allowing the home to easily shift from its five-bedroom scenario to a three-bedroom dwelling with a separate two-bedroom dwelling (scenario A) or a four-bedroom dwelling with a separate one-bedroom dwelling (scenario B).

In scenario A, the main-floor bedroom, conceived as a second master suite that was ideal for aging in place, is connected to the lower →

Previous Pages
Full House, by Leckie Studio, is surrounded by a screen of dark-stained cedar battens.

Designed to be used by three generations, this home features a courtyard which cuts through the center to bring in nature and light.

Left
In its default mode, Full House is a five-bedroom home, but can be easily transformed into three different configurations.

Right
The living space, built as one long line, can be shared by all generations.

Left
Maple trees grow outside the glazed interior courtyard.

Below
A close connection to nature brings the cyclical nature of the seasons to the fore.

ground. The idea was that the grandparents, who weren't interested in the ubiquitous aging-in-place basement suite—"I think the comment from the grandfather was, 'I didn't work my whole life running my dental practice to live in my son's basement,'" Leckie says—could easily host guests in the adjoined lower level without disturbing the rest of the family. In scenario B, the grandparents can remain in their main floor suite sharing living space with the young couple on the upper floor and the fully independent lower level suite could house the now adult children of the couple during their university years or should they return to the nest. When the adult children have their own children, the house can cycle back to its default scenario, with the young family living on the upper level, the great-grandparents remaining in their main floor suite and the original couple, now grandparents, can live in the basement suite. On and on, the home can shift in a continuous loop.

No matter what area of the home the generations are currently occupying, there is a strong connection to nature throughout. The glazed interior courtyard brings in light and ventilation, provides a clear sight line from the front yard to the backyard and, at its exterior section, is home to maple trees that allow the family to be aware of the changing of the seasons. "When you create an awareness in your daily living space of the cyclical nature of seasons and time, it starts to create a different awareness of aging if you will," Leckie says. "I really think that the more we're connected to an awareness of time, the more we understand that we're part of something larger." Three outdoor spaces—including a sunken courtyard at the lower level, a deck off the main level and a rooftop deck—create further connection and opportunities for privacy. "We really have these three discrete outdoor spaces that might help support the needs of three different generations," Leckie says.

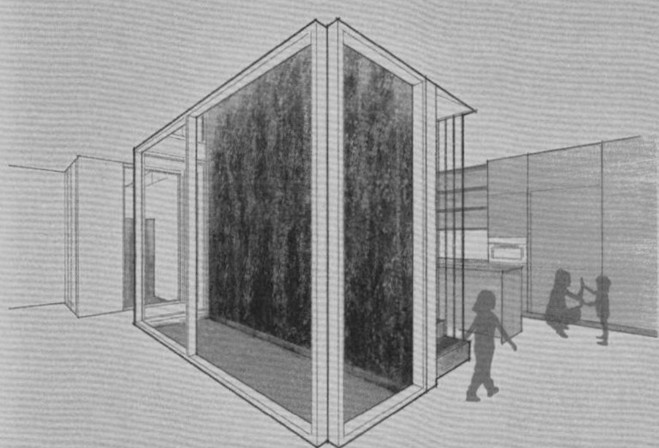

Like the home's cladding, these spaces are done in cedar so they will weather and patina, which Leckie encourages the generations to embrace.

"The idea of something being worked in, and the beauty of it and the way it is affected by time and inhabitation is much more soulful than the alienating aspects of newness," Leckie says. "I'm looking forward to the wrinkles that this house will get over time." •

"The majority of housing seems to be developed only with resale in mind, rather than the idea of growing old in a home."

A Space to Take Care of Each Other

Project

Housing Complex in Niigata

Designer

Schenk Hattori Architecture Atelier

Location

Niigata, Japan

For this project, Housing Complex in Niigata, the architects were tasked to create a new extension for three generations living in a typical Japanese housing situation. The home comprises two floors; bedrooms are on the ground floor, while the kitchen and living areas are upstairs. A pale wood interior with structural beams on the roof exposes the natural beauty of the home, an inviting space that is both modern and traditional. The varying textures of the wood lend the house an elegant simplicity. For privacy on the ground floor, the firm has reinterpreted the traditional shoji by utilizing a wall of glass windows on the exterior and lining them with translucent sheets of paper on a latticed wood frame on the inside. Although opaque, shoji diffuse sunlight into the house and provide visual movement from outside, like the swaying silhouettes of trees in the wind. Bedrooms are sparsely furnished, keeping in line with traditional Japanese minimalism.

↑ ↑ Communal Space

Every square meter is accounted for, including the in-between spaces of the interior surfaces, which are used for storage or extra seating. The resulting effect is warm, elegant, and functional.

←

Private Space
Bedrooms feature sliding doors and opaque shoji walls; translucent sheets of paper on a latticed wood frame. Shoji provides privacy yet still permits natural illumination into the home throughout the day.

→

How It All Works
The home's form plays with length to create a harmonious living environment. It consists of overlapping areas that accommodate multiple activities and functions, from sleeping or studying to meals and leisure.

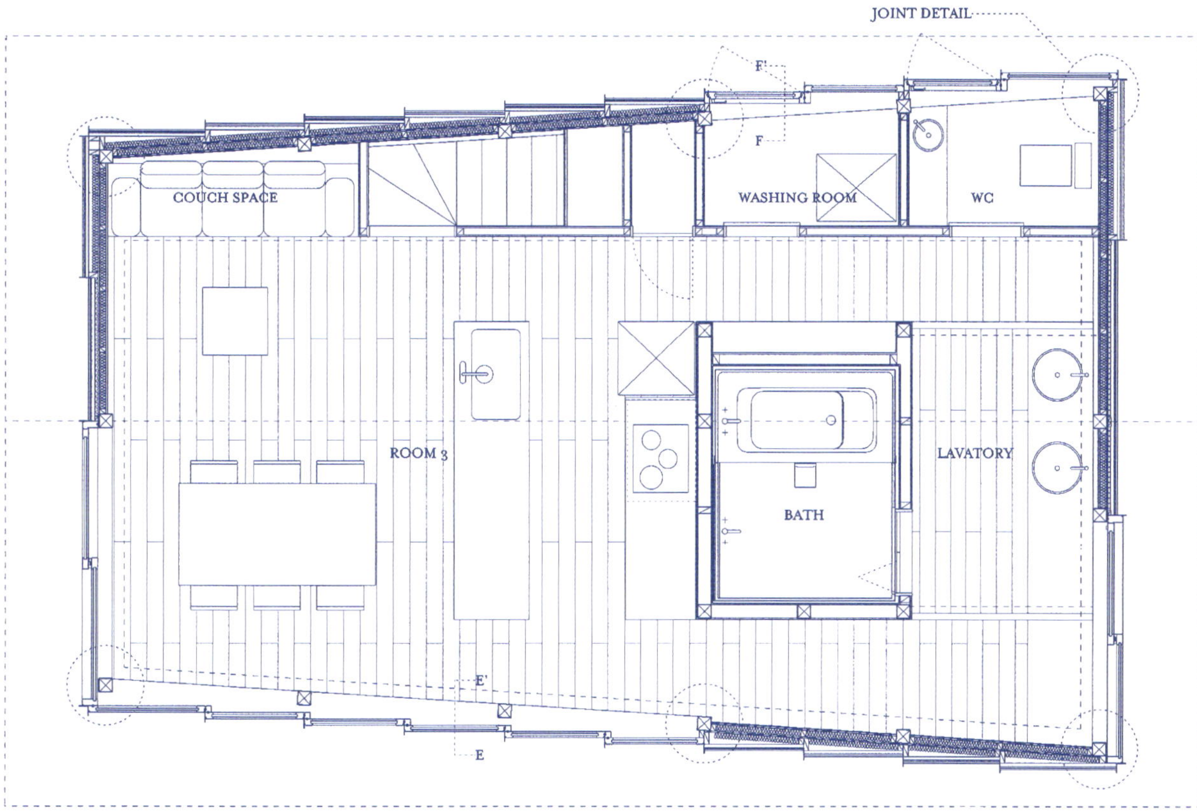
JOINT DETAIL
F'
F
COUCH SPACE
WASHING ROOM
WC
ROOM 3
LAVATORY
BATH
E'
E

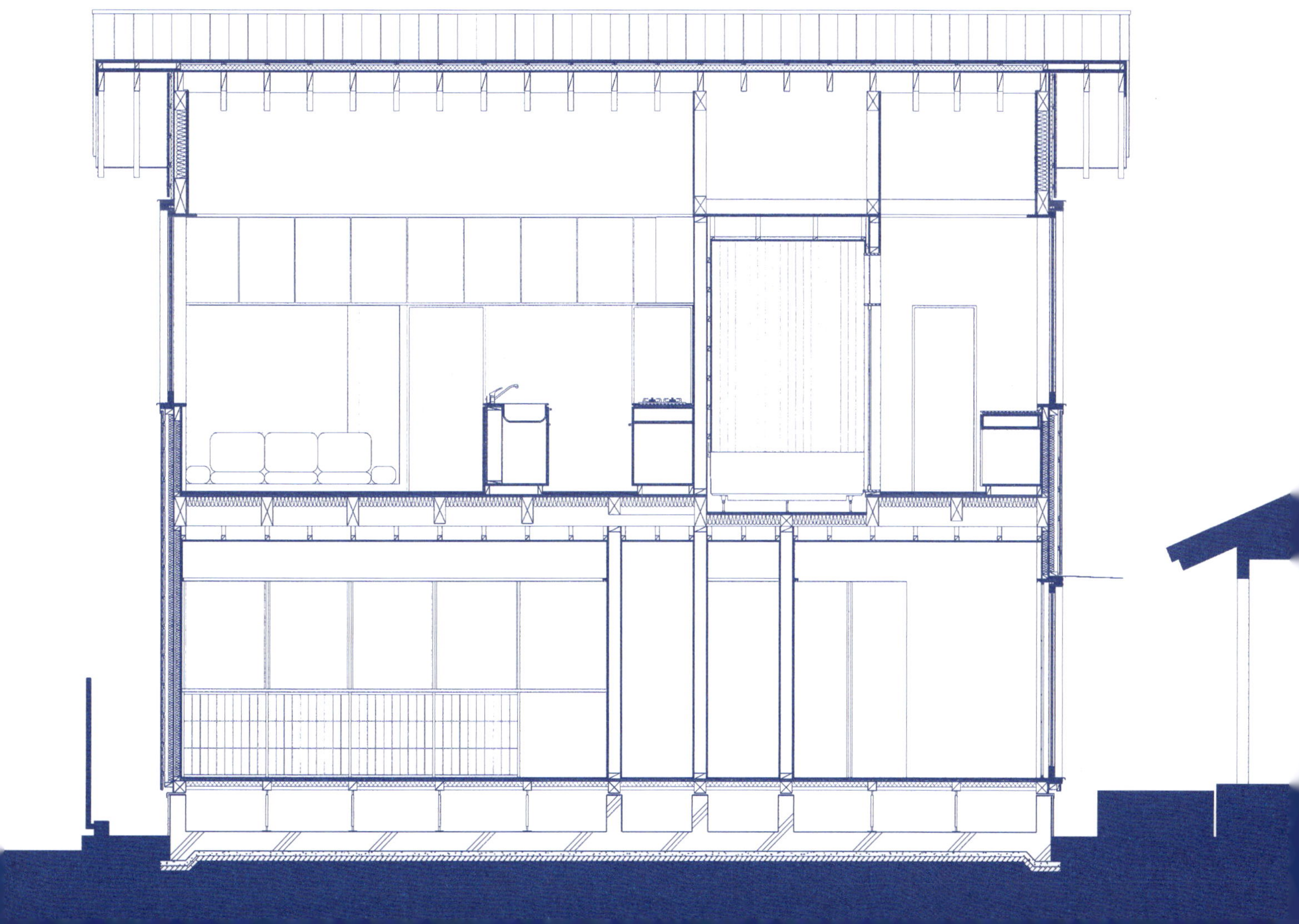

One Roof Houses Four Generations

Project
Home for 3 Households

Designer
FujiwaraMuro Architects

Location
Nagano, Japan

Modernity and privacy are the defining features of Home for 3 Households, which is occupied by three close-knit generations—the clients, their children, their grandmother, and their uncle. The project resulted from the clients' desire to tear down and rebuild their grandmother's and uncle's house, so that they could move in and live together agreeably. The front of the building has a stately, all-black facade, save for two narrow rows of windows separating the three floors. Despite its dark-presenting exterior, the home's generous use of glass on the inside soaks up an abundance of natural light. This is further enabled by two voids at the center of the home, linking each of the floors together. Made from glass panels, the voids allow light and ventilation to flow through the home, while giving the interior a more expansive feeling. A stainless-steel kitchen and contemporary furniture give the space a modern and clean-lined aesthetic.

↑ Communal Space
Given the home's position within a dense residential neighborhood, one of the priorities was to ensure the clients received as much natural light and ventilation in their home as possible. As such, the best solution was extensive use of glass.

↑
Communal Space
The living room, kitchen, and dining areas are located on the second floor for everyone to use. It has a stainless-steel kitchen island that facilitates social interaction.

↓

Connections
The home's contemporary design, with voids linking each of the floors, enables family members to live together under one roof, while also establishing three separate households.

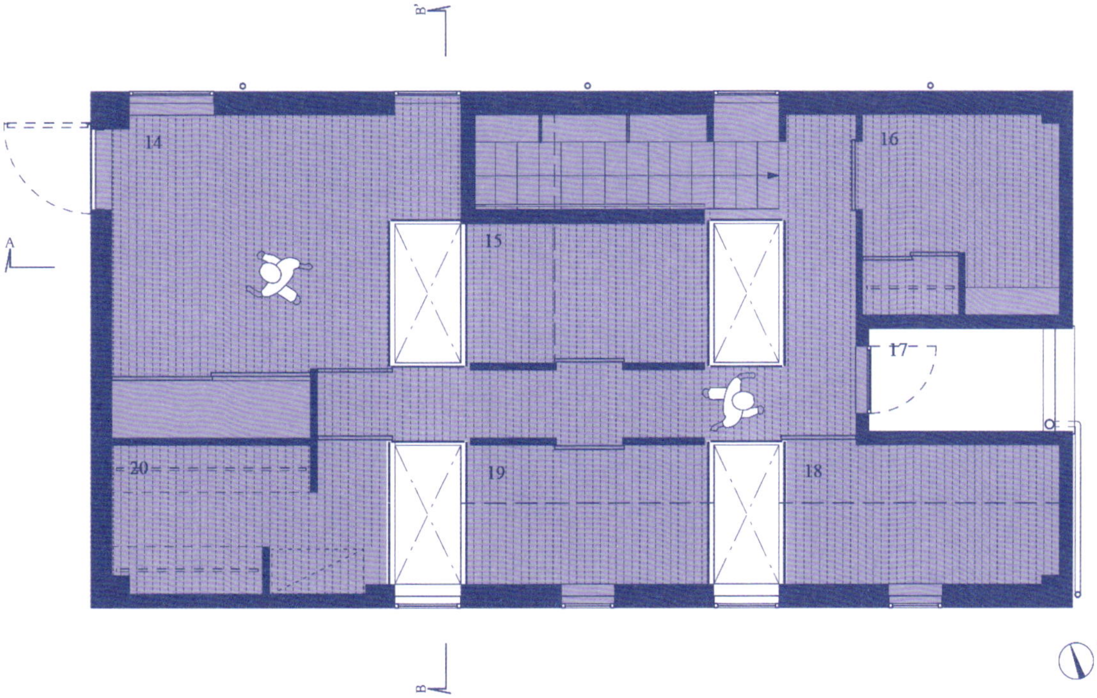

14. Bedroom
15. Kids room 1
16. Reading room
17. Balcony
18. Kids room 2
19. Kids room 3
20. Walk-in closet

0m 1 2

3rd floor plan

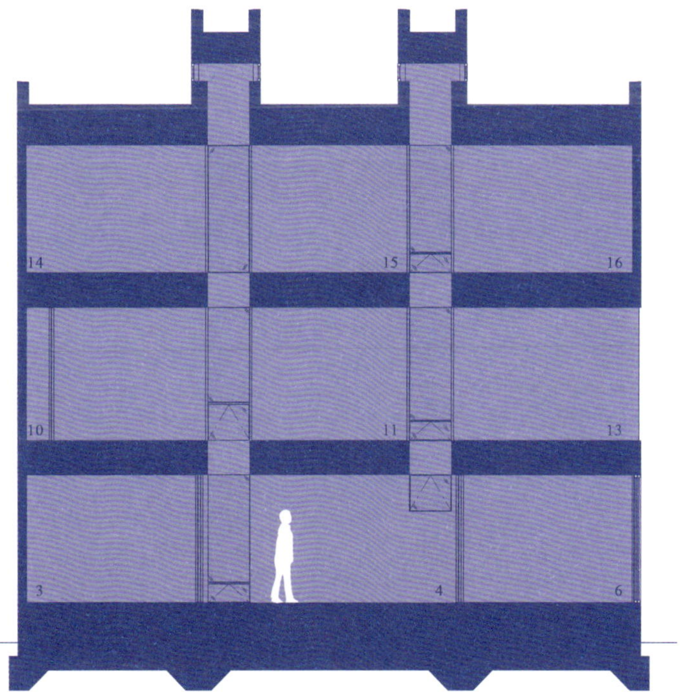

3. Entrance
4. Kitchen 1
6. Room2
10. Living room
11. Work space
13. Dining&Kitchen
14. Bedroom
15. Kids room 1
16. Reading room

0m 1 2

A-A' Section

↑ →

How It All Works

When creating the floor plan, the architects considered ways in which the residents would be able to sense one another's presence while occupying different areas across the multiple levels.

←

Private Space

Each room is separated by glass to give the space a more expansive feeling. On the third floor, the children each have their own little zone, which can be accessed by a step ladder from the hallway.

Prioritizing Green Spaces in Vietnam

Project
Wall House

Designer
CTA Creative Architects

Location
Bien Hoa, Vietnam

The defining feature of this airy, light, plant-filled house is not its double-height ceilings, modernist material palette, or expansive use of green trees, all of which are striking attributes in themselves, but rather, the stately and intricate brick facade, which is constructed entirely from perforated bricks salvaged from nearby building sites. Thousands of red bricks were punctuated with four small holes and stacked inconsistently at different angles which, beyond providing an interesting aesthetic, has a functional purpose: to generate fresh air for the family and natural light from the outside. "Our discussions with the client pointed to the idea of a house which is able to breathe 24/7 by itself," the architects explain. Trees and plants are dotted around the periphery of the home to create a garden oasis for three generations of this family to enjoy. The home provides ample space for the two parents, their two children, and their grandmother and grandfather to live independently, alongside each other, in a pared down and contemporary setting.

↑ Communal Space
Greenery extends outside of the home and continues behind the perforated brick walls.

← ↓

Communal Space

Quality air circulation throughout the house for family members and their pets was an essential criteria in the design of this project.

→

Connections

There are two important elements to the home's design: the brick wall, which prevents pollution from the outside entering in; and the abundance of greenery, which promotes healthy living environments.

A Vertical Forest in Vietnam

Project
Bamboo House

Designer
VTN Architects

Location
Hồ Chi Minh, Vietnam

With its narrow form and abundance of bamboo-filled planter boxes, Bamboo House aims to respond to the rapid urbanization of Vietnamese cities. Due to a lack of space and connection with nature, homes in this context have diverged from the low-density tropical spaces they once were. This house is part of a project aiming to reinstate verdant greenery into Hồ Chi Minh City's slim alleyways, which the firm says creates a more welcoming entrance. "The client's love for bamboo and its high relevance in the Asian context resulted in a facade covered with bamboo plantations." From the street, the planter boxes are positioned at zigzagging intervals up and down the five-story property, yet their deep eaves allow the windows to be kept open even during the rainy season and still let natural light inside the home. The green spaces also keep the house cool at all times, reducing the need for air-conditioning. The client, who is happy with the outcome, "feels like [their home] is a jungle in the middle of a bustling city."

↑ → **Communal Space**
The living room is fronted by large concrete planter boxes filled with bamboo, which improve the aesthetic quality of the home while also providing shading and privacy.

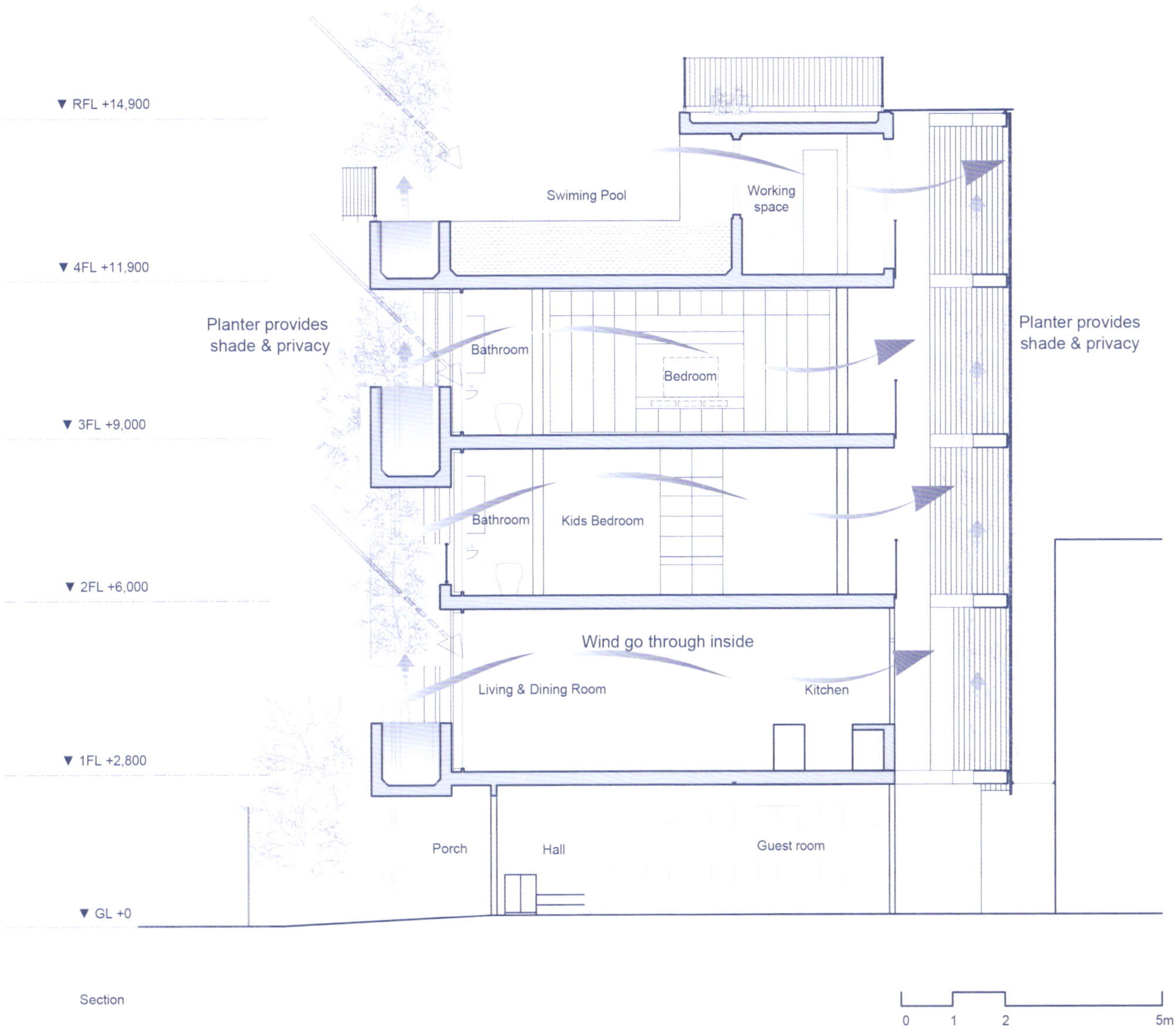

Section

← →

Private Space

Despite the limited size of the site, bedrooms follow a similar layout to one another across the floors, while spacious they are also sparsely furnished.

↑

How It All Works

Planter boxes are featured across five stories, from front to back. They bring natural ventilation throughout the home all year round.

Informed by Nature and Light

Project
Noble House

Designer
Apollo Architects & Associates

Location
Kanto Area, Japan

The architects of Noble House in Tokyo aimed to design a contemporary home that would stand in stark contrast to traditional neighboring residences. Harmoniously balancing minimalism and modernism, the design responds to the client's wish for a modern, urban home that could offer respite from the demands of everyday life. With its lush, almost resort-like atmosphere, this multigenerational home features a walled-in garden surrounded by an open-plan layout that accentuates the connection between inside and outside. Tall, concrete walls wrap around the property, ensuring security and privacy to create an inner world—without blocking any natural light from entering the home. The ground floor is dedicated for the client's mother, with a tatami room and study space alongside the pared down living and dining area. Dark wood flooring and exposed wooden ceiling beams lend the interior a rich tone, creating a welcoming mood that continues outdoors.

↑ **Communal Space**
The ground floor of this modern home was created for the client's mother and includes her bedroom and a tatami room. The second floor features the open-plan living area for all to enjoy, including a balcony and an interior terrace.

←
Connections
Stairs connecting the two floors employ a similar dark wood to the exposed ceiling beams, matching that of the veranda and terrace, which further blends the exterior with the interior.

→
Communal Space
The interior and exterior blend together through glass walls and terraces, allowing the extended family to make use of their private walled-in garden whether from the inside, or seated outside.

CREATING CONNECT-IONS

Centered around an interior courtyard, this modern-meets-rural home connects four generations through accessible spaces for all.

Song House, a striking white concrete home located in the Fengxian suburb south of Shanghai, has a full wheelchair accessible ramp wrapped around its exterior, embracing the home in a zigzag hug. Balconies and cutouts break up the mass, including a central atrium that opens up to the sky and features the family name inlaid in stainless steel on the floor.

"When you're standing in the courtyard, you can feel the whole building is a part of you, and you can feel the harmony between nature and yourself," says Zhang Lei, founder and principal of AZL Architects, which designed the three-level home for four generations. Surrounding this sacred space—once a tradition in Chinese homes—are interconnected private and public spaces that connect the family. "Each generation has their individual space and they also have their public space, bonding them together," Lei says.

Lei met the client—Lao Song, a retired electrician—through a Shanghai-based television program called *Dream House*, which connects selected members of the audience with an architect. Song and his wife had their eyes on returning to relaxing rural life after years in the city, and wished to build a home that could accommodate his elderly mother, in her eighties, his daughter and son-in-law and their daughter, as well as the parents of his son-in-law who have health issues. "[The client wished to create] connection between the old generation and the young generation," Lei says.

Replacing the dilapidated home where Song grew up and which his mother was still inhabiting, the multigenerational home is divided into three interconnected parts. Each allows the different generations to have their own private space and their own shared space, which flows continuously from one to the other. Incorporating small openings in between the two connects the three parts of the building and its residents. "There is a very strong connection between the public space and the private space," Lei says.

A key feature of the design is its suitability to elder residents with impairments. The ramp that winds its way around the house to the ground floor offers a fully accessible means to access different stories and additional outdoor spaces for the entire family. "We had to consider accessible design for the whole building," Lei says. At ground level, the south side is dedicated to Song's mother. Her bedroom, with an adjoined bathroom including a specially designed shower that makes caring for her easy, is adjacent to a shared living room. In between the two rooms, the first of three small cutouts, "we call them observation windows," Lei says, allow for easy checkups and communication between family members.

On the other side of the atrium, which brings in sunlight and natural ventilation, is a shared kitchen where the younger generation can use the gas stove and Song's mother can use her preferred wood burning stove. In the backyard, she can tend to the garden. "So she can live here, and cook, and do all her activities on the first floor," Lei says. →

Previous Pages
The house accommodates multiple generations, including the owner's 80-year-old mother.

A wheelchair accessible ramp wraps around the home's bright, white exterior.

Left
A soothing interior made with smooth cement and rustic furnishings offers a relaxed, rural ambience.

Left
Observation windows, partially visible on the top right, allows for easy connection and care between the generations.

Upstairs on the second floor, the bedrooms for Song and his wife and their daughter's in-laws are next to one another on the south side. Along with a wheelchair-accessible bathroom, an additional living room allows space for the two couples to connect without the sometimes wheelchair-bound in-laws having to go downstairs. Another observation window between the two bedrooms and one between the in-laws' room and the living room offer further points of contact, as do mirrors placed in stairwells and hallway corners.

A long set of stairs from the ground floor—where a long, thin skylight above the stairwell brings in additional light—leads to the younger generation's space on the north side including a master bedroom on the second floor with another set of stairs leading to the granddaughter's bedroom just above. Back on the second floor, a third set of stairs leads to a third level media room and a ping-pong room for the children.

Throughout the house, a soothing interior of smooth cement creates the relaxed rural ambience that Song was seeking. For the architect, the home is not a one-off, but a prototype study of "the rural city house," he says. A response to the rising costs of the city and the decline of rural villages, Song House—later used by Lei as a prototype for a residential planning project—connects the urban with the modern, the young generation with the old and eight family members inside one bold dwelling that stands out against the changing landscape. •

"The client wished to create connection between the old generation and the young generation."

Left
A central atrium opens up to the sky and the family name is inlaid on the floor.

A Tribute to Modernism in India

Project
Residence 1065

Designer
Charged Voids

Location
Chandigarh, India

Among the many projects designed by Swiss architect and giant of twentieth century architecture, Le Corbusier, was the master plan for the city of Chandigarh, India. Thus, it seems natural that decades on, local architects continue to draw inspiration from his legacy as a modernist visionary for their own architectural works. Residence 1065 is an expansive home in the style of Le Corbusier, with its dramatically cantilevered curved roof visually referencing the nearby Palace of Assembly. Three generations of the same family live in this spacious five-bedroom home; a couple with their two children and their grandparents. "The concept of the project is an attempt to alchemize eastern spatial planning and western aesthetics," explains the firm. As is typical of modernist architecture, asymmetrical composition, a generous use of concrete and glass, and an emphasis on open-plan geometry are features that characterize the impressive home.

→ →

Connections
A white, double-height cylindrical tower holds the puja room, a family space for prayer or meditation, with window openings made from geometric cutouts.

↓

Communal Space
With its expansive use of glass, the contemporary home connects the residents to the surrounding courtyards. For mobility reasons, the elderly members live on the ground floor.

A Triangular Ode to Modernism

Project
Tower House

Designer
Romi Khosla Design Studios

Location
New Delhi, India

A six-story modernist-inspired home in South Delhi makes excellent use of its wedge-shaped plot, measuring just 16 feet (5 meters) wide at the front and 70 feet (21 meters) at the rear. The innovative design provides an architectural solution for a couple, their adult children and spouses, and their elderly grandparents to occupy one floor each, while having space leftover for communal living on the ground floor. This follows a long tradition of joint family living in India, while providing private spaces that enable a shift away from traditional social structures and rituals. Each floor has its own balcony and living space, yet movement between floors is designed to encourage exchange between all occupants of the home. A material palette of exposed brick, steel, concrete, glass, and teakwood louvers define the home's modernist feel; and primary colors were used to paint the walls of common areas of the house, further referencing principles of modernist design.

↑ ↑ Communal Space
The lounge area has ceilings that are double in height to create a lofty living space. The use of teakwood louvers for shading and privacy add complexity to the home's modernist aesthetic.

↑ ↗

Connections

The family wanted a space that would encourage the children to put down their screens and focus on family time. The large living area, with its generously-sized couches, helps to achieve this.

↓
Flexibilty
Each floor was conceived to be self-sufficient and flexible in order to accommodate the changing needs of the family. While a standout criteria was to encourage social exchange between the generations.

Centuries-Old Multigenerational Living

In Asia, the tradition of multigenerational living dates back centuries, but today's dwellings are updated for contemporary lifestyles.

Located in Bangkok, Thailand, ReGen House was commissioned by a man who, following the birth of his daughter, wanted to live closer to his parents. He also wished to have a place that could accommodate his daughter's future family, should she also want to be near her parents when the time comes. "The question was whether or not it was possible to create a home that brings back the comfort of traditional Thai houses to the modern context," says Ekaphap Duangkaew, founder of EKAR Architects, who designed the home for four generations. The resulting house takes on a L-shaped footprint, with its main floors elevated above ground level to connect with the parent's house next door via a shared garden courtyard filled with greenery and trees.

Long before Bangkok was established, Duangkaew explains, Thai people lived in large families including grandparents, the younger generation, their children, and sometimes even uncles and aunts. "This way of life influenced the architectural design of Thailand," he says. A traditional Thai house is composed of several small, detached houses—each housing a smaller family—built around a central courtyard that connects the groups. The homes are built on poles allowing wind to flow through to lower the temperature, as well as protect from floods and wild animals. "We embraced the concept of traditional →

"A lot of the family values come from Confucius principles and that dates back to fourth century BC."

Previous Page
This modernist-inspired home in New Delhi follows a long tradition of joint family living in India.

Top Left
Located in Bangkok, Thailand, ReGen House reinterprets the traditional Thai house.

Bottom Left
ReGen House connects a son and his family to his parent's house through a shared garden and courtyard.

Thai architecture through the planning," says Duangkaew. "The attempt is to enhance living quality as well as family relationships."

From Thailand to India to China, Asia—speaking mainly to Southeast Asia, East Asia, and South Asia among its five subregions of which the countries in each are said to share "some degree of similarity" in terms of household, family, and marriage systems—has a tradition of multigenerational living that dates back centuries. Although it has certainly evolved, it's a tradition that continues to distinguish the continent from other parts of the world. "A lot of the family values come from Confucius principles and that really dates back to the fourth century BC, so that's literally thousands of years ago. [They] stress the importance of strong family loyalty, and also subordination to elders, also wives to husbands," says Dr Chia Liu, a postdoctoral researcher at the University of St. Andrews, whose research on coresidence among families in Asia shows that although Asian households and families are changing, multigenerational living continues to be widespread. "So this is how the societies were organized during that time."

From what is today China, these ideas spread to other Asian countries such as Japan and Korea, as well as Vietnam and other countries in Southeast Asia. "So you'll see some sort of similar family values in these areas," Dr. Liu says. Distinctions, which also exist within some of the countries themselves, are marked by gender differences in terms of who lives with parents. While countries like Thailand and Cambodia have bilateral family systems, where either a married son or daughter might reside with their parents to offer care, the majority of Asia is patriarchal, including the practice of patrilocality where, following a woman's marriage, she moves in with her husband who still lives with his parents.

In Tokyo, architect Tomomi Kito designed a house for a young couple with a child, the wife's parents, and her grandmother. Involving the renovation of an existing two-level timber home where the wife's parents had been living, the design focused on creating connection between the generations. "The primary concept of the house is to connect everyone under one roof," says Kito, "so the spaces basically seamlessly connect." Private rooms, which can also be exchanged among family members, →

Top Right
Cornwall Gardens House by Chang Architects, Singapore, is a verdant home to a couple in their sixties, three adult children, and the grandparents.

Bottom Right
Noble House by Apollo Architects & Associates is a multigenerational home in Tokyo, which has a strong indoor-outdoor connection.

are located along the common spaces including living rooms, dining rooms, and kitchens on both levels. "I wanted to have common space that all the family members can use," says Kito. "And in that place I want them to actively communicate regardless of the generations."

The younger generation's reasons for wanting to live together with their elders—including childcare help and financial benefits—speak to a changing cultural landscape beyond traditional filial piety for multigenerational living in Asia. Along with families pooling their resources in response to housing affordability and availability, particularly in an urban setting, and a shift from mere elderly care to grandparents offering childcare help as well, Dr. Liu also notes a lag in government response. "So there's a sense of filial piety [in the culture]—[that] people should take care of their elders, there's family interdependence," she says, "and then there's also sort of a policy failure, where, throughout the years, even though these countries have developed economically, the governments really haven't stepped up on old age care, so the countries are still expecting the family to take on that responsibility."

Following World War II, Japan was among a number of countries in Asia that, due to rapid urbanization and a rising economy, saw a decrease in household size—leading to the eventual rise of the nuclear family in the seventies—and a desire for more privacy. This has caused a decline in multigenerational living in Japan and in other economically strong countries like South Korea and Taiwan. Yet despite smaller family sizes and strong economies, Asia still shows a higher percentage of multigenerational living compared to other geographies around the world, and very few people with relatives living alone.

Changes in gender roles have also had an effect. Traditionally, women have been expected to act as the caretaker for both the young and old. But as their lives have become equally busy as mens' it's no longer feasible for them to carry on with previously expected duties, so grandparents, for example, are now helping with childcare.

Just as household roles and compositions are shifting in Asia's multigenerational households, so, too, have the homes accommodating them. In Singapore, where the once widespread kampongs—clusters of thatched-roof timber homes on stilts—housed extended families under one roof before they were eventually dominated by mass housing, Chang Architects has designed a generous, green-filled garden home for a couple in their sixties, their three adult children, and the grandparents, now in their eighties.

"Due to the differences in living habits and lifestyles of different generations [in modern Singapore], multigenerational living seems to be appealing and more successful in landed houses: houses where you own the land the house sits on," says Yong Ter Chang, founder and principal of the firm. "These houses [often multistory, imply more space] and rooms for spatial organization; whereby private spaces and social realms can be effectively configured for harmonious living." →

Top Left
House for 4 Generations by Tomomi Kito Architect & Associates in Tokyo was designed to create a connection between the generations.

Top Right
Private rooms, located along the common spaces, can be switched among the family members.

Bottom Left
A changing cultural landscape beyond filial piety brings families together in Asia for multigenerational living.

Distinguished by its terraced roof gardens and lush inner foliage, the four-level home wraps interior spaces around a central pool including inward-facing bedrooms whose steel mesh peripheries—forming interconnected planting verandas with foliage spilling over tiered decks—offer a visual connection across the home. "My client had plans that when the children get married, this house would offer them an option to stay on with their spouses, and to raise their kids here," says Yong Ter.

Though the tradition of multigenerational living continues to shift and adapt to current lifestyles, its long ingrained place in Asian society keeps the practice carrying on through the generations with architects responding with homes to accommodate it. •

"The attempt is to enhance living quality as well as family relationships."

Championing Wellness for Four Generations

Project

Cornwall Gardens House

Designer

CHANG Architects

Location

Singapore

This impressively verdant property, Cornwall Gardens House, was designed for a Singaporean family spanning four generations as an open concept home with an abundant amount of foliage and water, "making it a cool tropical paradise for the family," the architects say. A series of six bedrooms, multiple dining areas, a library, and a gym are some of the luxurious spaces that converge in a U-shape around a central swimming pool and a landscaped seating area, featuring a tree at its center. Other highlights include a waterfall, a koi pond, and a stepped roof garden with cascading vine leaves that flow down from one floor to the next, providing endless opportunities to connect with nature. The grandparents' room is located in the southern wing of the house, while their grandchildren sleep at the northern end: the two generations can reach each other via a bridge. The family were pleased not just with the functional and aesthetic aspects of the home, but also with the emotional and spiritual aspects it has come to enhance.

←
Private Space
Just like other areas of the house, the bedrooms look out over the pool and tropical gardens. Vines growing from one floor to another provide a touch of privacy and protection from sunlight.

→
Sustainability
The home promotes greenery, natural ventilation, insulation, and passive cooling in an ecologically friendly environment that evokes the mood of a rainforest or an oasis.

← ↑

Connections

Walkways that connect each section of the house are expansively lined with different plant species, including ferns, passion fruit trees, and climbing vines.

Adaptable for the Next Generation

Project
Daita 2019

Designer
Suzuko Yamada Architects

Location
Tokyo, Japan

In a residential area of Tokyo, this three-story house is designed for a family of three generations with changing needs. This adaptability is quite literally displayed through the home's flexible layout: two balconies on the second floor, held up by scaffolding, create an inhabitable frame of steel platforms that can be reconfigured as the family sees fit. "Each of the five members of the family has a different rhythm of life, so we designed the house so that each of them can live freely," the firm says. The home, Daita 2019, was inspired by an experience one of the architects had while visiting Rwanda, where she saw wild mountain gorillas in their natural habitat create overlapping and intersecting homes amidst the trees. Without separation from one another or from the terrain, the gorillas "formed a comfortable density that can be called a house." Similarly, the layout of Daita 2019 has no clear divisions, balancing openness and privacy through the steel construction that connects the garden to the inside at different points.

↑ → **How It All Works**
The three-story house and its gabled roof are clad in corrugated metal, except for the section of scaffolding. Steel pipes and platforms make up balconies, shelves, and stairwells.

← ↓
Communal Space
The interior includes staircases and exposed wooden structural features that create layers and distinct spaces, without the need for clean, bare walls.

→
Connections
With its multiple, linear passageways and staircases, the architects aimed to create a place where the residents could converse easily wherever they are.

←

Flexible Design
By obscuring the view with intersecting poles and panels of wood, the home balances openness and privacy, and can be modified depending on the mood of the residents.

← ↑ ↘

Private Space

Work and rest areas are separated from communal areas, yet they do not have solid walls or doors that close them off from each other or the nature surrounding the home.

A Retreat Revealing Luxury Interiors

Project
Creek House

Designer
Faulkner Architects

Location
California, CA, USA

Creek House, set in the Californian wilderness near Lake Tahoe amidst a field of volcanic boulders and a pine and fir forest, was designed for a multi-generational family whose primary residence is New York City. Each family member provided input into the design from suggesting finishes to tonal qualities. A simple brief directed the entire layout of their home: "don't hurt the boulders." Thus, both the site and every single boulder, even the car-sized ones, were left as found, with the impressive home built around them. The home cleverly cantilevers over several boulders, building up layered spaces across the site that allow for privacy. While indoors, a brutalist-inspired design champions a material palette of concrete, steel, and wood, with expansive windows that reveal tranquil nature outside. Enhanced by natural light and shadow, the home was inspired by an essay on Japanese aesthetics called *In Praise of Shadows* by Junichiro Tanizaki.

↑ How It All Works
It was important for the clients that the architects' design did not disturb any of the natural landscape, so the house moves around and alongside the boulders and trees.

← ←

Communal Space
The modern home has plenty of nooks and comfortable areas to relax amidst the mountainous terrain, surrounding forests, and rock gardens.

↓

Material Palette
Concrete, steel, and glass are the predominant materials, with fire-resistant steel rainscreens, tempered glazing, and concrete walls protecting the home from the elements.

↓

Connections

The house is split across two levels. As members walk along the stairs, a dramatic drop in the topography is revealed through the windows displaying impressive boulders.

→

Private Space

When they visit for holidays from New York City, the family enjoys quiet living in harmony with nature and natural light.

The Multigenerational Experience

Residents of multigenerational living configurations open up about what it's like to live together.

For British Columbia, Canada-based Matthew Heinl, his wife Kaylin, and his parents, the decision to share a home together—along with two children, two dogs, two cats, and five chickens—was one they made together. By that point, Matthew's recently retired mother Anne was commuting back and forth from the nearby town of Sidney every day to take care of her two grandchildren.

As the city, Victoria, grew increasingly expensive, the option for the older generation to buy something closer wasn't affordable. For that same reason, the younger generation couldn't afford to renovate their existing home either, but they loved their neighborhood and wanted to stay. Pooling their finances, the two generations made a plan to tear down Matthew and Kaylin's old house and build a shared house on the same plot. "We just started talking about it and looking at numbers. And it just made sense," says Heinl. "We're big believers in a family unit that is stronger together than apart."

Sharing a home comprised of two volumes joined together by an airlocked walkway, with the younger family in the larger side and the older generation in the slightly smaller one, the Heinls, like many families living in multigenerational properties, are benefitting from more convenient shared care, shared costs, and more time together. The arrangement allows family members to relieve some of the burdens of life, to give one another a break, to easily lend a hand. Interdependence can actually lead to more independence. Living side by side comes with the comfort of knowing someone is there. →

1427

"The kids see their grandparents more, they're more active in going over there, even for just an ice cream. It's just more time together."

Previous Page
Designed by D'Arcy Jones Architects, Double Header House was designed for three generations to live in.

Top Left
Two volumes, joined together by an airlocked walkway, form a home for the Heinl family in British Columbia, Canada.

Bottom Left
Anne Heinl in her kitchen. The family also includes two dogs, two cats, and five chickens.

It offers the opportunity to build richer relationships and make the most of precious time together with aging parents and grandparents.

"The kids see their grandparents more, they're more active in going over there, even for just an ice cream," says Kaylin. "It's just more time together." "As a family," adds Heinl.

The family gather for family dinners about once a month on the larger side of the house, along with birthdays and Christmas. "Now, my dad can have his dinner, say his hi and then go back to his privacy and Mom can stay and have a glass of tea or wine," says Heinl. Ula, their 7-year-old daughter, appreciates the arrangement as well. "I get to come over and have a sleepover and movie night with my grandparents," she says.

Spontaneous sleepovers and family gatherings have also been a benefit for Vilma Melasniemi whose own family plot in Helsinki, Finland, has supported multigenerational living through the years. "Actually, all of us got married in the garden or in the old house," says Melasniemi, referring to her parents' 100-year-old home where she grew up with cousins, family friends and, for several years, her maternal grandparents living in the home's upper level apartments. "As well, Maila's [my paternal grandmother's] funeral was held in my parent's house. It's a long and nice history around the place."

In 2010, Melasniemi and her husband Juho made the decision to build a family home on the plot with an apartment for her grandmother on the ground level. "She was living in Helsinki, by herself, but on the fourth floor with no elevator. I used to go there for a coffee, take her to shop, and help her to clean every now and then," Melasniemi says. Her parents funded the 270-square-foot (25-square-meter) apartment. "Maila loved flowers, so we had the idea she could enjoy the garden," says Melasniemi. Aged 91 when she moved in, Maila got cancer the same year and passed away sooner than the family had hoped. But Melasniemi's father got to spend his last days with her. "They drank whiskey and talked about life," Melasniemi says.

Today, her cousin's daughter lives in the apartment, but it's always available for Melasniemi's two children who have fond memories of →

growing up alongside their grandparents. "We spent Christmases at our grandparent's house. After we moved next to them I could stay as long as I wanted to and didn't have to go to sleep if my parents already left," says Melasniemi's daughter Aamu, who is now 20 and lives in the city center. She recalls the convenience of running over to her grandparents' house if she didn't have something and the comfort of knowing they were there, "As a kid, it was very special to have sleepovers; say good night and in the morning, be together with the family."

Anne Heinl believes the key to making multigenerational living work is respecting one another's boundaries. "If you're going to live like this, I think the big thing is you have to respect each other's space. You're not living together [per se]," she says. "We have our side, they have their side. I don't think it can be a free-for-all."

Melasniemi agrees. "My parents never come to our door just for fun. We live very freely our own lives here." But she appreciates the years of help they gave with childcare. "I think the relationship between my parents and my children is much richer than if we were not living so close." Now, as her father is having health issues that are taking a toll on her mother's time, it's their turn. "Sometimes she can go to do her own things when she knows we are around to help my father if needed," says Melasniemi, "so now we can give back something from what was given to us by this arrangement." →

Left
Kaylin and Ula, mother and daughter, in their kitchen. Ula enjoys being able to see her grandparents on a whim.

Right
The Heinls enjoy the benefits of shared costs, shared care, and more time together.

Top Left
Architect Makoto Suzuki and his wife look out at the view from their multigen live-work home.

Bottom Left
Also a weekend home for Makoto's father, the home includes studio spaces.

Below
The multi-volume home in Japan includes a studio space for their friend, sculptor Takenobu Igarashi.

On the island of Hokkaido, Japan, architect Makoto Suzuki has designed a harmonious live/work family home where he hopes to give something back to his friend and sculptor Takenobu Igarashi, and his father. Surrounded by forest, the timber home is made up of several adjoined volumes, along with his own home and studio, and a workspace for his wife, a studio for Igarashi, and a weekend home for his father.

"Igarashi had mentioned that he wanted to build a small studio, and I thought it would be a good inspiration for me and my staff if we could incorporate it into this home project," says Suzuki. "On a personal note, I wanted to be able to live with my father when he got old and before he passed away."

Now 84, Suzuki's father was living alone in Tokyo for a number of years following the death of Suzuki's mother in 2002. In 2014, he moved in with Suzuki's younger sister and her husband. "I didn't want to put the burden of care on my sister and her husband alone, so I came up with the idea of a home where he could spend time with us," Suzuki says. The architect feels that the home's strong connection to its tranquil surroundings "has been very helpful in stabilizing the mind and helping us to live together."

"We sometimes have a cup of tea together in the dining room with a view of the forest and talk quietly," says Suzuki. "He loves this quiet environment, watching the birds and small animals that come to the terrace. When I was a child, my father was busy working and I didn't get to talk to him face-to-face very often, so it's a very precious time for us."

Creating closer relationships is a benefit for all of the families. "It kind of bonded us," Anne Heinl says, over in British Columbia, Canada, "the whole building process and living together—helping each other, talking about issues, like, if there's an issue with the kids or the garden or a window, whatever, it's not just your opinion, you can meet as a group, and kind of get consensus."

Of course that doesn't mean the experience is not going to come without some ripples, but they are manageable. "It's not that hard, like there are rules, and there are going to be irritations, but it's really not that difficult," says Kaylin. "There's more than enough room for everybody." •

An Angular Home to Grow Old In

Project

House M-M

Designer

Tuomas Siitonen Office

Location

Helsinki, Finland

House M-M, an elegant four-bedroom home built for three generations, charms with its visually-striking untreated larch-clad facade that will adapt to Finland's nordic climate of varying weather and temperatures across seasons, changing patina over time. The Finnish owners, an actor couple, worked with the architects to design a unique-shaped angular home that could provide warmth and comfort to their young children and extended family. Also, it was important that the home be flexible as the family grows up. Thus, the children's bedrooms were conceived to also serve as future workspaces. Large windows in the living room and bedrooms, in differing shapes and sizes, look out onto grassed lawn and a garden of apple and lilac trees, enriching the owners' integrated relationship with nature. As well, a generously-sized terrace further enables this outdoor experience, with ample space to host friends.

↓ ↓ →

Communal Spaces

A second-story porch, an open-plan living and dining room, and a mezzanine living room area provide various common spaces for different ways to spend time together.

←

How It All Works
The uniquely-angled home has a roof that dips in the middle. For views of the expansive scenery around the property, the rooftop can be accessed via a ladder at the back of the house.

→ ↓

Private Space
The brief was to design an inspiring, functional, and environmentally sustainable house. Bedrooms have large glass windows with views of the surrounding trees.

An Inventive House of Stairs

Project
Stairway House

Designer
Nendo

Location
Tokyo, Japan

By far the most defining feature of this uniquely-designed home is its colossal steel and concrete staircase, which spills inside-out. Bright and open thanks to three stories of floor-to-ceiling glass walls, Stairway House cuts an imposing form, with its grand flight of stairs uniting each level. The faux staircase, too steep to safely use for its intended purpose, starts in the back garden, penetrating the glass-walled rear facade and continuing up to the top floor. Not just a connecting architectural element, the gray steps provide space for plants, house secret bathrooms, storage, and cupboards, while a real staircase hidden inside its steel walls allows the elder family members to move with ease between the different levels.
In line with the firm's pared down aesthetic, the monochrome interior is sparsely furnished; most of the interior spaces are black, including the minimal kitchen, island bench, study desk, and other furniture pieces.

↑ **Private Space**
From the street, the house appears like a windowless white box, shutting itself off from neighboring properties. A thin, vertical opening allows light to seep into the interiors.

←
Flexible Design
The home, designed for the family of Akihiro Ito, chief operating officer at Nendo, features a real staircase, bathroom, and storage cupboards inside its colossal faux staircase.

← ↓
Communal Space
On the third floor, a study sits across the master bedroom. Each space has ample natural light and views of the trees in the backyard, which is connected to the interior via the staircase.

←

Connections
More than just a connecting architectural element from inside to outside, the gray steps provide space for storage. A door hidden underneath the exterior staircase leads inside.

↓ →

Communal Space
Typical of the design firm's style, interior spaces are ultra-minimal, with pared down rooms and designer furniture. The ground floor has views of the generations-old persimmon tree.

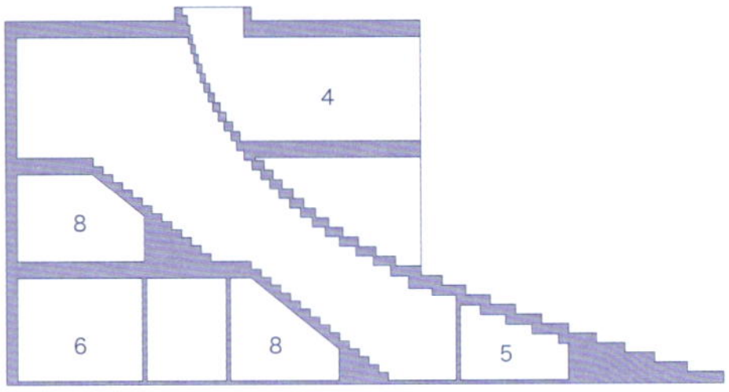

1 LIVING/DINING ROOM
2 KITCHEN
3 BEDROOM
4 STUDY ROOM
5 CAT ROOM
6 BATHROOM
7 TOILET
8 STORAGE

SECTION

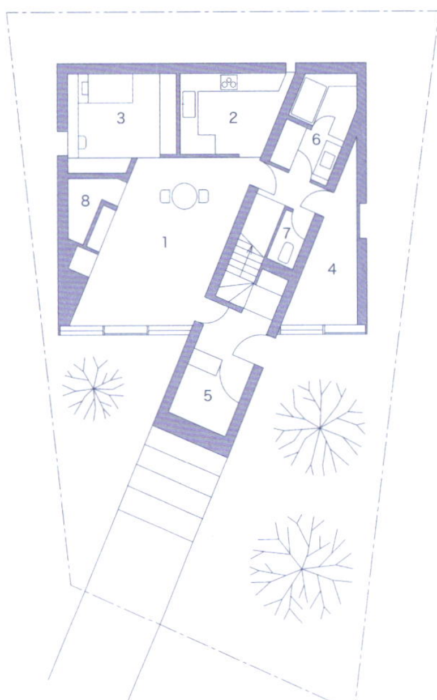

1 LIVING/DINING ROOM
2 KITCHEN
3 BEDROOM
4 STUDY ROOM
5 CAT ROOM
6 BATHROOM
7 TOILET
8 STORAGE

1F PLAN

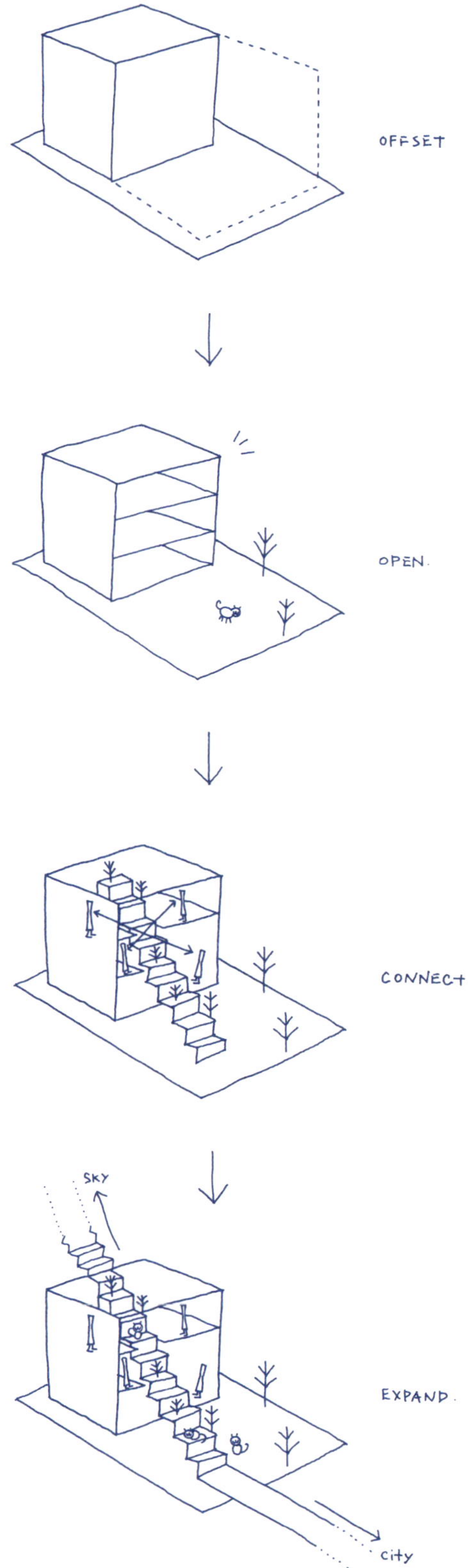

↑ ↗ →

How It All Works

The aim was to connect the different floors, as well as the inside and outside, through a multifunctional step-like object that goes well beyond superfluous decoration.

TWO

Designed as two houses in one, this boat-like home was designed to allow four generations to live together and apart.

BECOME

ONE

20

This long and narrow house in Vaux-sur-Mer, France, is home to a family of boating enthusiasts, who can gaze out over the sea from the home's south-facing windows. "When you are standing on the first floor you can see the sea everywhere," says architect Marie Périn, a partner at TICA architectes et urbanistes, which designed the two-level home to accommodate up to four generations.

Clad in a mix of zinc and white concrete panels, the house appears as one home on this solar-gaining side. On its north-facing side, a nearly uninterrupted line of zinc cladding with the exception of polycarbonate at a midpoint, the home reveals itself as two houses in one.

"[The client] asked us to think about how we can build a house that gives the family the opportunity to be together when they want to be together," says Périn, "and to be separated when they want to be separated."

Commissioned by a retired couple, the home was designed to accommodate the couple full-time and their children, grandchildren, and parents during frequent visits. Comprising a 1,700-square-foot (160-square-meter) side and a 1,000-square-foot (100-square-meter) side joined together by shared space in the middle, the bioclimatic home replaced their existing home on the plot that couldn't comfortably accommodate the whole family.

"They told us about their experiences. It was sometimes difficult to live together in the same house," Périn says. "Because they were really honest. We understood it, [and] we transposed it into the space."

Defined by its warm wood interior of exposed structural cross-laminated timber (CLT), the home is bookended by living rooms on both sides of the ground floor, with a small open kitchen in the smaller side and a larger kitchen with built-in wood shelving—on both the inside and outside—in the larger side where a ground floor bedroom →

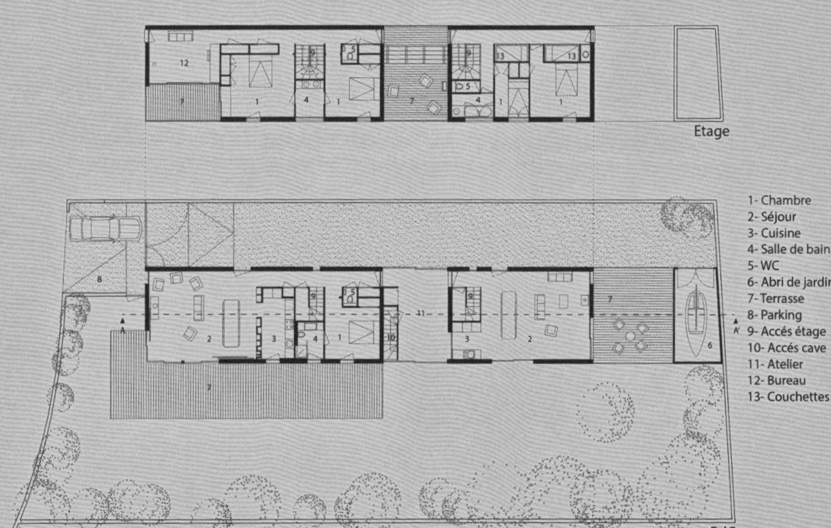

Previous Pages
The stairs of the shared rooftop terrace doubles up as seating.

On its zinc-clad north-facing side, this home reveals itself as two houses in one.

Left
The home's smaller side, 1,000-square-foot (100-square-meter), features a small, open kitchen.

Right
Shared space in the middle brings the family together while dividing the house into two.

Right
The children can run from one side to the other with ease. Sliding doors can open out the space even further.

Left
A warm wood, made of exposed structural cross-laminated timber (CLT), creates a cozy and modern interior.

Left
The boat-inspired home offers open spaces for the family to connect.

is certified as fully accessible. Upstairs on both sides a variety of bedroom types are located—from the master suite with its own terrace and a double bed on the one side, bunk beds, and double beds on the other—that can easily accommodate short or longer stays, growing grandchildren, and visiting friends.

"There is not a designated room for each child, everyone is free to choose the bed suitable to their stay," Périn says. Noting that the second house doesn't have to be heated if no one is there, she adds, "if only one child or one grandparent is coming, they don't have to open the second half because they have enough beds to welcome them in the first house."

Shared space in between, including a ground floor workroom—a place for shucking oysters, storing sandy beach items, or hanging laundry—a cellar for wine and food below it and an upper level terrace with stairs that can double as seating, acts as an acoustic barrier and a cross-over point between the two sides.

On both levels, long corridors running the length of the north side of the house create a line of connection. "The idea was to have a visual relation between the two houses," Périn says. On the upper level of one side, the corridor provides a place for berth-style beds for the grandchildren's friends.

Back downstairs in the shared workroom, a straight line from east to west offers additional ventilation when the sliding doors are left open and a connection to the outside where two outdoor terraces provide space to gather or retreat. From the terraces on the upper level of the south side, the family can look down at those gathered in the back terrace as if on a boat.

While the private terrace adjoined to the master bedroom offers the couple a space to be alone, the younger generation can gather with friends on the garden terrace on the other end of the house—both not visible to one another.

"The house has allowed all the generations with their way of living to be able to find their freedom without disturbing the freedom of others," Périn says. "I think all families have problems, and perhaps people don't see each other because of that. Because when they do the space is not according to how they live and how they want to live," she says. "This house is really thinking with that point of view." •

"We were asked to build a house that lets the family be together when they want to be together, and be separated when they want to be separated."

Dynamic Home for a Large Family

Project
Charles House

Designer
Austin Maynard Architects

Location
Melbourne, Australia

Charles House, with its contrasting shapes, angles, textures, and materials, is a distinct piece of residential architecture. The multigenerational home was designed for longevity for a family of five, plus grandparents, that they could live in for at least 25 years. The brief was to create a practical and low-maintenance house and garden with five sections, filled with natural light, multiple garden spaces, and ponds, bridges, and water features. "Multigenerational housing is a double-edged sword," explain the architects. "It is wonderful ... a diverse family home is often a healthy family home. However, [it] also reflects the nature of our economy and the consequences of housing unaffordability." The home therefore aims to facilitate a support network for each family member, from childhood to later in life. With its interlinking volumes of varying proportions, the home playfully eschews any predictability in form, with each block clad in different slate patterns.

↑ **Sustainability**
With its bulk insulation, solar array, and water collection, this home is one of the firm's most sustainable. Windows feature external blinds and awnings that help minimize solar gain in the warmer months.

← ↓

Communal Space

The garden wraps around the entirety of the house, making it visible from almost everywhere inside the building. The hope is that it encourages the children to engage more with nature in their backyard.

→

Connections

The master bedroom, walk-in closet, and ensuite are physically separated from the rest of the sleeping quarters but accessible via a small bridge. The external slate cladding is continued inside.

↑ →

Private Space

Upstairs, the children's bedrooms are accessible to each other via a sliding wall. Each of the sleeping spaces can be opened or closed according to changing ages, functions, and desires.

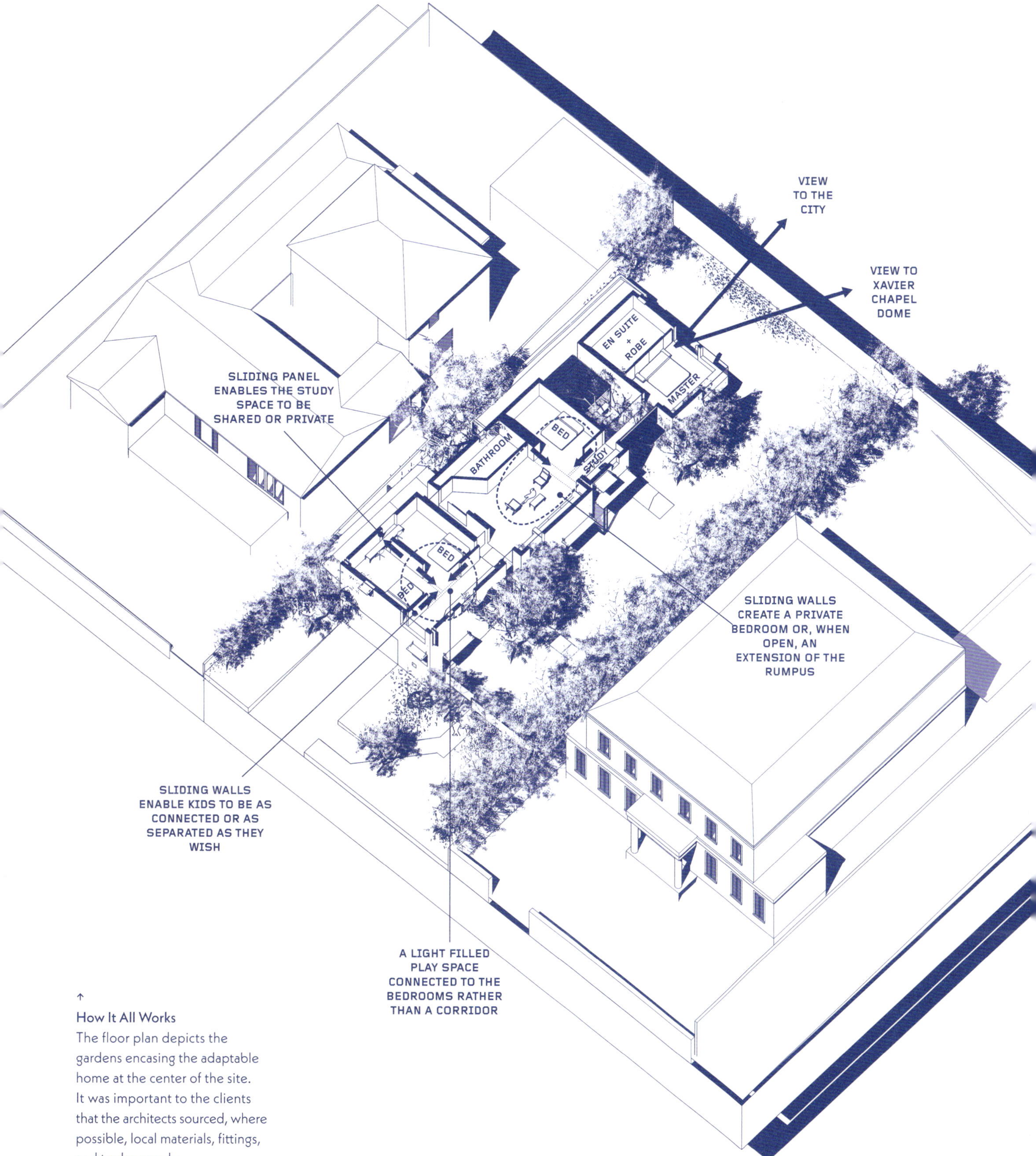

↑

How It All Works

The floor plan depicts the gardens encasing the adaptable home at the center of the site. It was important to the clients that the architects sourced, where possible, local materials, fittings, and tradespeople.

An Australian Family's Resourceful Addition

Project
House 3

Designer
Coy Yiontis Architects

Location
Balaclava, Australia

The homes that architects design for themselves often present a fascinating glimpse into their experimental minds. From the street, House 3 appears like its Victorian weatherboard neighbors—but behind the heritage facade lies an ultra-modern extension comfortably fitting a family of eight: two parents, four children, and two grandparents. Strict space requirements in this part of the city mean that considered planning is needed so that every square meter is used with intention. The house is therefore divided into two buildings—old and new—that are separated by a large central courtyard and pool. Appearing much larger than it actually is, the extension of House 3 presents a geometric facade at its rear, with long windows jutting out of the angular timber-paneled exterior. Partners in life and business, the architects share the belief that residential properties in cities need to accommodate a sense of spaciousness while still providing occupants with privacy.

↓ → →

Communal Space

While this home is not extra large, and with the arrival of the home-owners' fourth child, the design plan nonetheless successfully accommodates this family of eight.

←
Connections
The architects found an inventive way to build an extension. The solution was a new two-story timber-clad building encasing a central courtyard and pool.

Reimagining the Australian Dream

Australia is a hotspot for multigenerational living, with forward-thinking architecture offering a fresh take on the form.

Australia has long been known for its single family suburban homes and detached megahouses. Homeownership is part of the Australian dream. But, as the cost of living keeps rising, this lifestyle is becoming increasingly unattainable. As a result, Australia is experiencing a remarkable rise in multigenerational living.

Younger generations are either choosing to stay in their parents' homes or returning home as boomerang children after stints away. But it's the country's rising elderly demographic, with people over 65-years-old making up 15 percent of the population in 2017, who are not surprisingly the fastest growing age group for multigenerational homes. The quality of care for the elderly—made glaringly visible during COVID-19—leaves many families longing for better care options, or choosing to provide it themselves.

"The rise of multigenerational and coliving environments reflect the wider pattern of Australian households adapting to population growth, housing affordability and changing lifestyles," says Melbourne-based architect Matt Gibson. As one of the world's most culturally diverse populations, Australia's emergence as a kind of epicenter for the rise of multigenerational living is also influenced by people bringing their cultural tradition into the country as they emigrate to it—particularly Asian immigrants and their subsequent generations.

In light of these issues, multigenerational living is a solution that makes sense for some, but for many—motivated by the benefits of shared space, shared care and time spent together—it's a lifestyle →

"The rise of multigenerational and coliving environments reflect the wider pattern of Australian households adapting to population growth, housing affordability, and changing lifestyles."

Previous Page
In Melbourne, this vertical home houses a couple, their three adult children, and their partners.

Top Left
This adaptable home by Matt Gibson Architects includes space for the whole family on the first floor.

Top Right
The residence is topped by a shared retreat and terrace level.

Bottom Left
One for each member of the family, the studio apartment-like bedrooms are spread across two floors.

choice they're happy to make. According to the Australian Housing and Urban Research Institute, one in five Australians were living in households with more than one generation in 2006. Those numbers are one in four in Sydney. Around the country they're predicted to keep growing.

Architectural experimentation is creating space for a new expression of multigenerational housing in the western context. Whether the lifestyle is motivated by necessity or choice, architects in Australia are embracing this way of living through clever, good-looking design that supports it.

In Sydney, Emili Fox, who codirects Sydney-based architectural firm Fox Johnston, shares the upper two levels of her breezy courtyard home with her husband and two children, while the lower ground level incorporates a guest suite for grandparents and an adjacent one-bedroom apartment—currently rented out to a young couple. "I wanted to design a house that would be flexible for us now, and also flexible for us in the future," Fox says. "I wanted to have a series of spaces that we could rent out in the interim, and it would also work for my parents, now in their seventies, to stay in the long-term if they needed to live with us."

Designed to capture airy views and light, Ballast Point House—defined by its Western red cedar batten cladding and courtyard garden—is perched on a ridge with separate upper and lower level entries. "We're on a very compact site, which means the house is very vertical," Fox explains. "So what that means is you end up having very distinct, separate areas. We can very easily have ground floor, upper floor living, and bedrooms, and then you can have separate apartments on the lower floor, so the site sort of lends itself to that."

The adjacent one-bedroom apartment, which has tall ceilings and split levels between the living space and the bedroom—currently separated by a joinery cabinet at what Fox refers to as a secret door—has been rented out to a young couple for more than a year. "We know them well now and have drinks or dinner with them from time to time," Fox says. Today, Fox's parents use the guest suite every two →

weeks or so. But with provisions for a lift and the ability to fully connect the space to the main house, the inviting area—including a bathroom, kitchenette, and balcony—can become a full-time home for either of the couple's parents, if needed. "It would be nice for them not to have to go into a retirement home for as long as possible," Fox says.

Along with the idea of creating a flexible space, Fox's appreciation of the Asian tradition of multigenerational living influenced her decision to design the home. "The family unit is considered a positive generational model rather than the elderly being outsourced," she says.

This tradition also came into play at Charles House, a multigenerational home designed by Melbourne-based firm Austin Maynard Architects for a family of five with roots in Vietnam and China. "So there was a cultural connection there," says architect Andrew Maynard, principal at the firm, of the family's decision to commission a multigenerational home.

A series of connected volumes clad in patterned slate and timber, the Melbourne-based residence incorporates a flexible, accessible space on the ground floor that can be easily adapted into a fully equipped flat for a set of grandparents from its current use as a music room and recreational space.

"The space is easily transformed by sliding doors into a private space for a grandparent to inhabit," says codirector Mark Austin, "but is still connected." →

Left
Architect Emili Fox, of Sydney-based Fox Johnston, designed a flexible multigen home for her family.

Right
On a compact side in Sydney, Ballast Point House incorporates a guest suite and adjacent apartment on its ground level.

Left
Charles House is one of several multigenerational homes by Austin Maynard Architects in Australia.

Below
At Charles House, a recreation room easily adapts into a granny flat on the ground floor.

Citing rising real estate prices as a factor, the firm has had numerous requests for multigenerational homes of the same nature. "The family are physically closer," says Austin, adding that one great house is more affordable than two, "at some distance apart."

In St Kilda, an inner seaside suburb of Melbourne, a four-story residence made from ten zinc-clad boxes was designed for a couple and their three children: one teenage daughter and two adult children who each live with their partners. Simultaneous separation and connection have also been incorporated into the design by Matt Gibson Architecture + Design, but of a wholly different, vertical variety. Set in an urban infill lot in a mixed-use zone, the adaptable home, including a required commercial space with a separate entrance, rises up into a first floor communal area for the family followed by two floors of studio apartment-like bedrooms: one for each member, two on each floor. The residence is topped by a shared retreat and terrace level.

"This adaptable, mixed-use and vertical living type creates another avenue for family members to stay together longer while providing a level of independence in the building configuration," says Gibson. For the family, the home offered an opportunity to live together longer with the conveniences and amenities of city living and a level of quality the family's young adults wouldn't otherwise be able to afford. It was also an opportunity to challenge Australia's traditional quarter-acre block housing typology, known as the suburban subdivision, that they'd come from.

"This pattern of urban settlement is still very popular, but as Australian cities are becoming hugely populated, architects are looking for denser patterns of settlement that still create the amenity that the quarter-acre block offered," Gibson says. "In this particular circumstance, but also as a model for future flexible adaptable housing in cities experiencing rapid population boom, it seems to add to and aid coliving-type scenarios," he says. "The young adults can feel like they're checking into their own self contained unit or even hotel-like living space, yet with all the benefits or shared resource and family support."

Gibson's design and others are proving that the Australian dream of homeownership doesn't have to fade into Australia's past. It just has to change form. "As a species we've always lived in complex villages in different ways. This sort of modern way of living where it's the nuclear family and you get to a certain age and you leave and you make your own nest, that's actually quite a new invention," says Andrew Maynard. His firm appreciates the idea of returning to this former, it takes a village way of living, albeit updated for today. "We like the idea that you go back to a more complex way that the family can exist," Maynard says. "And it's a lovely way to live." •

A Holiday Retreat in Nature

Project

Sorrento House

Designer

Cera Stribley Architects

Location

Sorrento, Australia

In the popular seaside town of Sorrento, along Victoria's stunning Mornington Peninsula, a former 1960s home originally designed by modernist architects McGlashan Everist has been given an upgrade by Cera Stribley. The existing layout, considered progressive for the era in which it was built, was left largely as it was, with slight alterations to suit contemporary beachside living. A home away from home, Sorrento House is often inhabited by the client and their mother, who stays in the guest wing near the front of the property. The grown children and their families regularly visit on week-ends, enjoying water sports from the little jetty connected by a stairway from the deck. The home's new interior woodwork is one of its most striking features, which keeps in line with the original design's existing colors, timbers, and joinery. With its mid-century aesthetic, this 1960s home is updated for the twenty-first century with updates like hydronic heating and double-glazed windows.

↑ → **Communal Spaces**

The unbeatable ocean views means that the family regularly host gatherings on the deck in summer. Despite being designed more than 50 years ago, the home's modernist feel is as relevant today as it was then.

← ↑

Sustainability

The builder worked with artisan tradespeople to deconstruct and reinstall the timber boards back to their original position. A specialist painter restored the colors to accurately match the original wood.

→

Connections

The family come together at the kitchen, dining, and living areas at the back of the home. It was integral to the success of the building that the existing charm of the residence be retained.

LIVING ON THE LANE

Behind a breeze-block facade, this house acts as its own micro townscape, giving a mother and her son autonomy in their shared home in the suburbs.

The Mermaid Multihouse is encased in a porous facade of cement H-blocks, positioned to offer shade, security, and a through line for mitigated breezes. From the outside, the house looks deceivingly like a single family home. From its inside, it becomes clear the residence is in fact a duplex, albeit a new take on one: a dividing party wall is bordered by two external double-height arcades instead of indoor spaces. Being inside the home feels like being outside. "Instead of being in a little suburban thing where all you can see is the neighboring fence, suddenly you're in this urban thing where you can see very safely right out into the depths of your context," says architect Timothy Hill, founding partner of Partners Hill, the firm behind the design in collaboration with Hogg & Lamb.

Located near Mermaid Beach on Australia's Gold Coast, the house was an opportunity for a very typical demographic constellation in Australia—a baby boomer with property who was living alone in a former family house in the suburbs and a young adult who, thanks to the country's "spectacularly expensive housing," Hill describes, would have had to move outside of the city or into a highrise flat—to join forces and coinvest in a home that would allow them to stay in their community, benefit from each other's company if they were so inclined, and reap the rewards of what is ultimately two houses for the price of one.

"[That] means their lives are richer, either of the households can do household things, not just family things," Hill says. "It may involve long-term guests, tenants, working from home, consulting suites, big parties, all the things that go along with what a real urban life and a real life span is like." →

Previous Pages
A breeze-block facade is used for its form and function on this urban house in the suburbs.

With a gate at its entrance, this house was designed as a micro townscape for two generations.

Left
The lines between the inside and outside world are indeed blurred.

Right
The home's two kitchens look out onto the backyard, flanked by two flat-roofed gazebos.

Right
Two double-height arcades, separated by a party wall, are the dividing line which defines this duplex.

Left
Ventilation makes its way through to the private areas of the home thanks to the breeze-block facade and the arcades.

Below
The arcades create pathways and gathering places that border the private, interior spaces.

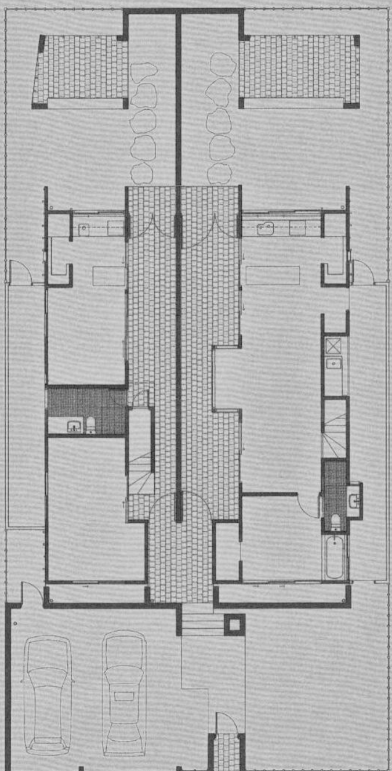

Designed like a "micro townscape," as Hill calls it, the two-level home starts at its front gate, which, past a plinth made of concrete blocks and over a timber walkway, leads to the double arcades on either side of the dividing party wall, where the terrazzo-clad pathways—glare-free, impromptu gathering space that's partially outdoors—are bordered by the enclosed rooms of each house and lead to a lush back garden with two flat-roofed gazebos on either side of the continuing wall.

"So it's very like a micro version of a nice street. There's a pavilion at the park at the end. There's a lovely gate at the start, and it has a choice of places along the way," describes Hill. Currently functioning as living space, bedrooms, guestrooms, and income-generating spaces (from office space to rentals), these so-called places along the way look out and down into the arcades, and benefit from light from three sides.

"By using a townscape model, rather than an inside-the-home model, the private spaces are really private, and the public spaces are very public," Hill says. Slightly different in size, each side is sparsely furnished and includes a kitchen that looks out to the backyard garden space. Upstairs, the rooms benefit from taller ceilings, textured walls, and plenty of light.

Thanks to the arcades and the security of the breeze-block periphery, windows can be left open in some rooms, a great bonus in the area's humid climate. "So much of the building will ventilate 24-hours a day," Hills says.

Built on a budget with a clever mix of affordable materials balanced with the bespoke block construction, the carefree, easily manageable home is a new typology that adds more depth and diversity of use to Australia's omnipresent suburbs and to the lives of the home's inhabitants.

"The fun is, that these two people who are otherwise destined to live in something by themselves now live on the edge of a tiny lane, which means, they can invite other people to be nearby," Hill says. "And the difference is, they haven't invited them into their home. They've invited them into their lane." •

"Suddenly you're in this urban thing where you can see very safely right out into the depths of your context."

A Modern Australian Abode

Project
Ballast Point House

Designer
Fox Johnston

Location
Sydney, Australia

Located right next to the waters of Ballast Point on the iconic Sydney Harbour, Fox Johnston celebrates multigenerational living with an imaginative design for Ballast Point House. The lush property belongs to the architectural firm's director, Emili Fox, who wanted a sustainability-minded home for her partner, their two children, and dog, Billie, as well as space, a guest suite, that caters to her parents. Perched on a cliff overlooking Mort Bay and the city, the impressive courtyard house is informed by the Australian landscape. Unfolding over multiple levels, the lower two floors are designed to be self-sufficient accommodation for family and friends, while the main residence stretches out over an additional two levels, complete with a balcony offering harbor views and rooftop cactus gardens. Interior courtyards and gardens blooming with plant life are clustered around the light-filled spaces, further bridging the natural and built environments, along with the home's soft color palette and relaxed indoor spaces.

↑ → Connections
The house is designed to work with the seasons. In warmer months, it is closed down during the day and opens up again when the temperature outside starts to fall, lessening the need for air-conditioning.

16

↑ → →

Communal Space

The brief was to design a "forever home" that could be a testing ground for the architect's ideas about living, while also provide her parents with an independent home under the same roof.

Reinventing the Suburban House

Project

RaeRae

Designer

Austin Maynard Architects

Location

Melbourne, Australia

In the Melbourne suburb of North Fitzroy, a case of lucky timing allowed a family occupying a single-fronted terrace house to buy the property next door and renovate the two to build a truly unique home. RaeRae retained the facades of the heritage-protected terraces, and features a defining zigzagging roof that meanders in a manner reminiscent of a mountain range, continuing down the entire length of the site and swerving around in a L-shape to the back of the property. The varying facade gives the impression of multiple individual volumes, but the home's interior is actually one open-plan space, which is ideal for this family of five. Instead of the usual request for a parental retreat away from busy shared spaces, the owners asked that the main bedroom be designed at the heart of the house. It is a "home for life, for us, and our family ... something that will be fun for our young kids today and equally fun for them in the future," the owners say.

450

← ↑

How It All Works

The dynamic home, comprising two properties side by side, converges around a central courtyard, with the living spaces all oriented towards a garden.

→

Connections
The home has much personality, with details chosen by all family members. A spiral staircase leads to a bathroom and three bedrooms, with a brightly colored carpet chosen by each child.

← ↓

Communal Space
The dining and living areas are functional, modern, and welcoming, with a home entertainment system and comfortable sofas in the living room for family time.

M

N

O

P

R

S

T

V

W

Z

Come Together

The Architecture of Multigenerational Living

This book was conceived, edited, and designed by gestalten.

Edited by Robert Klanten and Elli Stuhler
Contributing Editor: Joann Plockova

Introduction by Joann Plockova

Case Study and Feature texts by Joann Plockova:
pp. 24–31, 50–57, 76–83, 98–105, 132–139, 150–157, 180–187, 202–211, 224–231, and 236–243

Project texts by Steph Wade

Editorial Management by Sam Stevenson

Head of Design: Niklas Juli
Design and layout: Isabelle Emmerich
Cover design: Melanie Ullrich
Design Assistant: Antonia Heckenbach

Photo Editor: Valentina Marinai

Typeface: Neue Kabel by Marc Schütz

Cover photography by Peter Bennetts

Printed by Gutenberg Beuys Feindruckerei GmbH, Langenhagen
Made in Germany

Published by gestalten, Berlin 2021
ISBN 978-3-96704-004-3

Bibliographic information published by the Deutsche Nationalbibliothek. The Deutsche Nationalbibliothek lists this publication in the Deutsche Nationalbibliografie; detailed bibliographic data is available online at www.dnb.de

This book was printed on paper certified according to the standards of the FSC®.

FSC www.fsc.org MIX Paper from responsible sources FSC® C009051